Praise for *The* [

"*The Four Sacred Gifts* beautifully ███████████████████
the power to create a culture and ████████████████ ....
simplicity of the means to do this rings true, as do Anita's stories of
courage, strength, and inspiration. Now is the time to embrace these
gifts for ourselves and the world."

—Joan Blades, cofounder of MoveOn.org,
LivingRoomConversations.org, and MomsRising.org

"A beautiful answer to why so many people feel separate, alone,
and afraid, and how to get back naturally and easily into harmony,
connection, and love with ourselves, nature, and each other."

—Christy Whitman, *New York Times* bestselling author

"Not since Don Miguel Ruiz has there been such a powerful book!
A beautiful transmission of vital indigenous wisdom for our times.
These gifts from the elders, wrapped in stories of courage, resilience,
and inspiration, are a treasure to immerse ourselves in, and to pass on
throughout the world. A must-read for anyone wanting more from life."

—Teresa de Grosbois, founder of the Evolutionary Business
Council and #1 international bestselling author of *Mass Influence*

"Dr. Anita Sanchez reveals how ancient indigenous wisdom can
transform us today by helping us find our true purpose, heal past
hurts, and create deep connection."

—JJ Virgin, nutrition, fitness, and mindset expert, and
New York Times bestselling author of *The Virgin Diet*

"These four sacred gifts from the elders have the power to change
lives and heal communities. With deep personal courage and brilliant insight, Anita Sanchez leads the way."

—John Perkins, *New York Times* bestselling author of *The New
Confessions of an Economic Hit Man* and author of eight other
nonfiction books on global intrigue and indigenous wisdom

"Enlightening, illuminating, and inspiring. A gift for generations to come."

—Norbert S. Hill, Jr., Oneida Nation, prior Executive Director, American Indian Science and Engineering Society

"*The Four Sacred Gifts* liberates us to heal from the inside out and rediscover our deep connection to all life. . . . A powerful journey awaits you here, one of courage, resilience, vision, inspiration, and faith in your own power to live a whole and purposeful life."

—Natalie Ledwell, cofounder of Mind Movies and host of *The Inspiration Show* podcast

"*The Four Sacred Gifts* may be one of the most important books you will read in these times. With heartful generosity and authenticity, Anita Sanchez shares timeless indigenous wisdom using a simplicity and depth of language that resonates."

—Claude Poncelet, PhD, physicist and author of *The Shaman Within*

"No remedy is more needed in today's confusing and seemingly chaotic times than the power of simple wisdom. In this beautifully written book, Anita Sanchez draws on her own moving and revealing life experiences to present four gifts of indigenous wisdom that can help us heal ourselves, our communities, and our broken world."

—William Ury, coauthor of *Getting to Yes* and author of *Getting to Yes with Yourself*

"A true antidote for today's world of indifference and greed! *The Four Sacred Gifts* will leave you feeling inspired and prepared to immediately begin making a difference from the inside out."

—Bob Chapman, CEO of Barry-Wehmiller and author of *Everybody Matters: The Extraordinary Power of Caring for Your People Like Family*

"Dr. Anita Sanchez has written a soul-opening book with prose as light as a feather that reads like a warm embrace. More than just a good book, *The Four Sacred Gifts* awakens an inherent memory of how good it feels to be in connection with ourselves and the world."

—Deborah Sandella, PhD, RN, #1 international bestselling author of *Goodbye, Hurt & Pain*

"Through her own insights and personal stories, Anita brings to life the power and critical relevance of indigenous wisdom to our times."

—Robert Gass, cofounder of the Rockwood Leadership Institute

"A must-read primer for anyone considering indigenous wisdom written for modern times."

—Debbi Dachinger, host of the *Dare to Dream* radio show and bestselling author of *Wisdom to Success*

"A riveting read filled with relatable stories and ancient wisdom, it's obvious that Dr. Anita Sanchez put her life's work into this masterpiece."

—Marilyn Suttle, coauthor of *Who's Your Gladys?* and president of Suttle Enterprises, LLC

"A story of hope, and a pathway to the world we are waiting for."

—Cynda Collins Arsenault, cofounder of Secure World Foundation and Arsenault Family Foundation

"Anita holds a bright light and ancient mirror up to our true nature, inviting us to recognize and resonate with the wisdom of elders worldwide. She offers us her most practical and valuable methods, stories, and truths that carry a vibration of peace, which I believe will ripple into waves of compassion in unexpected and delightful ways."

—Ken Honda, #1 internationally bestselling author

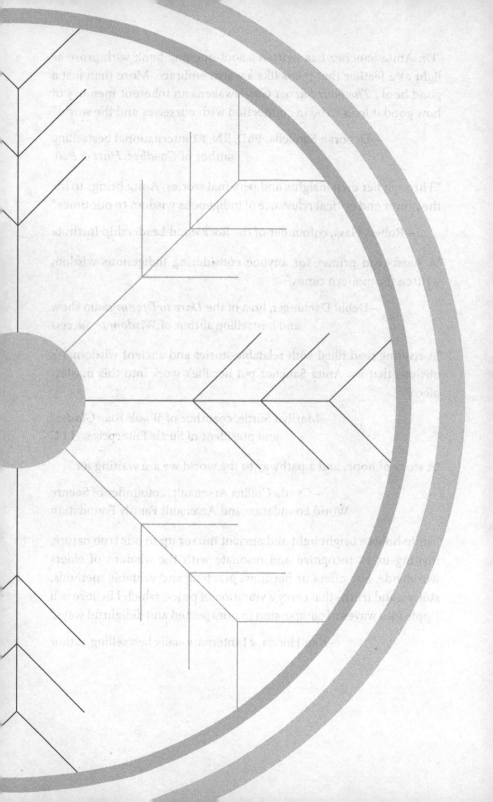

THE
FOUR SACRED
GIFTS

Indigenous Wisdom for
Modern Times

DR. ANITA L. SANCHEZ

ENLIVEN BOOKS

ATRIA

NEW YORK   LONDON   TORONTO   SYDNEY   NEW DELHI

ENLIVEN™
ATRIA

An Imprint of Simon & Schuster, Inc.
1230 Avenue of the Americas
New York, NY 10020

First Enliven Books trade paperback edition November 2018

This publication contains the opinions and ideas of its author. It is intended to provide
helpful and informative material on the subjects addressed in the publication. It is sold
with the understanding that the author and publisher are not engaged in rendering
medical, health, or any other kind of personal professional services in the book. The
reader should consult his or her medical, health, or other competent professional before
adopting any of the suggestions in this book or drawing inferences from it.

The author and publisher specifically disclaim all responsibility for any liability, loss or
risk, personal or otherwise, which is incurred as a consequence, directly or indirectly, of
the use and application of any of the contents of this book.

For information about special discounts for bulk purchases, please contact
Simon & Schuster Special Sales at 1-866-506-1949 or business@simonandschuster.com.

The Simon & Schuster Speakers Bureau can bring authors to your live event. For more
information or to book an event, contact the Simon & Schuster Speakers Bureau at
1-866-248-3049 or visit our website at www.simonspeakers.com.

Interior design by Kyoko Watanabe

Manufactured in the United States of America

10 9 8 7 6 5 4 3 2 1

The Library of Congress has cataloged the hardcover edition as follows:

Names: Sanchez, Anita L., author.
Title: The four sacred gifts : indigenous wisdom for modern times / Dr. Anita L.
  Sanchez
Description: New York : Atria/Enliven Books, 2017. | Description based on
  print version record and CIP data provided by publisher; resource not viewed.
Identifiers: LCCN 2017006931 (print) | LCCN 2017018616 (ebook) | ISBN
  9781501150876 (eBook) | ISBN 9781501150708 (hardback) | ISBN 9781501150869
  (paperback)
Subjects: LCSH: Indians of North America—Religion. | Indian philosophy—
  North America. | Indigenous peoples—Religion. | Conduct of
  life. | Wisdom. | Ethnophilosophy. | Traditional medicine. | Healing. |
  BISAC: SELF-HELP / Motivational & Inspirational. | BODY, MIND & SPIRIT /
  Inspiration & Personal Growth. | BODY, MIND & SPIRIT / Healing / General.
Classification: LCC E98.R3 (ebook) | LCC E98.R3 S26 2017 (print) | DDC 299.7—dc23
LC record available at https://lccn.loc.gov/2017006931

ISBN 978-1-5011-5070-8
ISBN 978-1-5011-5086-9 (pbk)
ISBN 978-1-5011-5087-6 (ebook)

To my mother, Frances Medina Sanchez, and my father, Phillip H. Sanchez, for giving me life.

To my husband, Kit Tennis, and my two sons, Alex and Nico, who bring me joy.

And, most important, to all the indigenous Elders who bring us their wisdom to help us fulfill our journey.

CONTENTS

CONTENTS

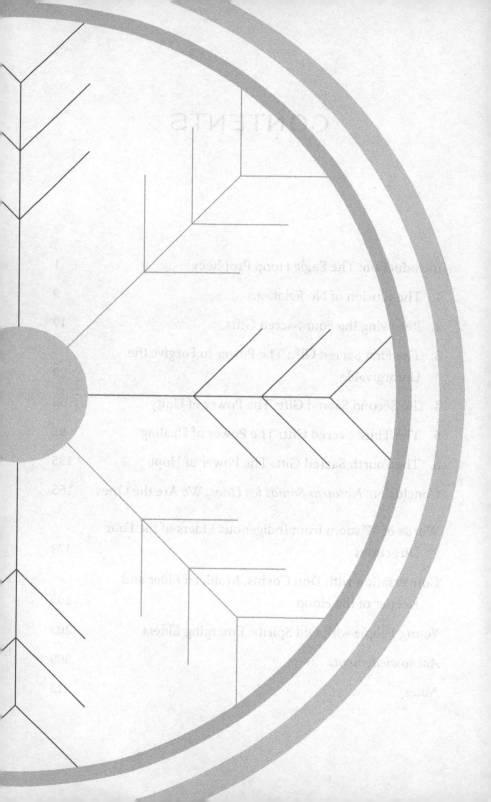

Introduction:
The Eagle Hoop Prophecy

The hoop is an evolving symbol for humanity, as its wisdom and presence reminds us of how to be and how to do.

—DON COYHIS, MOHICAN ELDER
AND KEEPER OF THE HOOP

IN 1994, A VISION came to a Mohican man as he slept in his house tucked into the large pine trees on the edge of the Rocky Mountains. An eagle flew above his sleeping self, dropping a beam of light upon the man's head. This ray of light began to expand, reaching from the sky to the earth.

Within the light, a very small sprout sprung forth, becoming a tree, growing through each of the four seasons—the spring, summer, fall, and winter.

Then the leaves of this tree began to fall off. And then soon, the branches began to fall off. What remained was a single stem of the tree, which rose up vertically and then turned horizontally, bending and forming itself into the perfect shape of a circle to represent the earth and the universe.

When the circle or hoop was completed, a single dot of light formed in the sky, coming down to the hoop. The dot of light transformed into an eagle feather attaching itself to the hoop. Then more and more dots of light came from all the four directions—north, east, south, and west—becoming eagle feathers, attaching themselves to the hoop until there were one hundred eagle feathers in all.

When an indigenous person seeks guidance, being in right relation with their community, they will naturally seek out the wisdom of the Elders, who are in communication with spirit and Mother Earth. So, with this dream, Don Coyhis, Mohican messenger, and members from his Turtle Clan took this vision to seventeen Elders in South Dakota, who said, "You need to build that hoop." They saw this vision as a prophecy of the coming together of the human race: "There is only one race, the human race."

The Elders said, "We walk around on earth in our earth suits. Some come in red earth suits, some white, yellow, and black. Take these four colors of ribbon and wrap each around the hoop, bringing them together in the middle, and joining them with one eagle feather in the center."

Listening to the Elders, they began to build the sacred eagle hoop. A willow branch was made smooth and gently shaped into a circle. They took the colored ribbon—red, white, yellow, and black—praying and wrapping each one around the hoop. They took their collection of one hundred eagle feathers, praying and attaching each one to the hoop.

Then there was a sacred gathering and hoop ceremony.

Twenty-seven indigenous Elders from the four colors and directions—Elders from the North American tribes representing the red and south direction, a Buddhist Elder from Tibet representing the yellow and east direction, a Sami Elder from Finland representing the white and north direction, and two Elders from African tribes representing the black and west direction—responded to the call.

During the ceremony, there was no man-made notion of time—past, present, or future; there was only the Now, one spirit, calling forth through the human beings, through their different languages, through their sacred chants, prayers, blessings, and meditations. There was no separateness, only one mind, one heart, one spirit connecting these Elders and their sacred traditions from the four directions.

The twenty-seven Elders, with joy and solemnity, took cedar planks, laying them in the four directions, placing the hoop on top, and saying, "We have come together. We will put into this hoop four gifts that are necessary for this coming together . . . this healing time.

"The first gift we place is the power to forgive the unforgivable.

"The second gift is the power to heal." The Elders prayed their healing medicines into the hoop.

"The third gift is the power of unity. The power to come together.

"And the fourth gift is the power of hope. The ability to dream, to see wellness and the powers to attain it."

After the sacred eagle hoop was built and blessed by the twenty-seven Elders with their four gifts, the hoop began a great land journey, traveling through thirty-five states in the U.S. and to Canada. Don Coyhis took the hoop and traveled to cities, communities, colleges, reservations, and homes. He traveled through many seasons, climates, and environments in this land of our ancestors.

And on this journey, an awakening began. A healing time of prayers, tears, hopes, and a creating time of dreams from all the people, indigenous and non-indigenous alike. Standing in a central place, the hoop is both symbol and catalyst to our awakening, which continues to unfold in magical ways as it makes its journey, touching so many lives.

The four colors, the four directions of the hoop, symbolize harmony and interdependence between the different peoples around the world. The hoop is meant to support all people to discover and trust the four sacred gifts, so that each of us can be a life-giving connection to others: all beings, earth, and spirit. The hoop is a powerful force, a powerful medicine, a coming together of the human race.

Momentum is building. A movement is building across our great lands. We are seeing with a clearer vision the strength and wisdom of our Oneness, and the gifts of the hoop are needed now more than ever to help us realize that vision of life.

WHAT IS INDIGENOUS?

Before we continue forward on our journey together, I want to take a moment to describe in more detail what it means to be indigenous, and in particular an indigenous Elder.

In the beginning, everyone's ancestors were indigenous. They were hunters and gatherers and lived in relationship to nature, to the earth. This is an anthropological definition of an indigenous person. If you search online, you will find that "indigenous" is usually described as: native or aboriginal or first peoples, who are the original habitats of a region or environment.

Now we have confused this term "indigenous" to mean someone who is born and raised in a particular place with other members of their tribe, therefore that makes them indigenous. But for many of us who have been separated geographically and/or culturally from our tribe's original or ancestral traditions and instructions, we then don't regard ourselves as indigenous.

Indigenous people are often defined as minorities. However, we are legally recognized as Nations in a country such as the United States, not minorities. Nations with rich cultures and knowledge, and with diverse traditions and practices. However, all of these definitions only touch the surface.

Across many indigenous peoples and their tribes, they point to a common description rather than a single definition, and that is: A truly indigenous person is one who has intimate connection with Mother Earth and who embraces all human beings in order to get along with them. There is a respect for diversity, which is part of the circle of life. Pluralism is valued, so it does not matter what color you are, for there is no being better than or less than, no negative judgment. We are all connected. Indigenous peoples listen to not only their minds but most importantly to their hearts and to what Mother Earth is saying. This description of indigenous people is what I hold to be true and what this book is based upon.

As for indigenous Elders, these men and women are "tradition bearers" and are recognized by their people, specific tribe, or culture group as having wisdom. An Elder is not necessarily a function of age. The Dalai Lama is an example of being an Elder as a child.

To many indigenous people, Elders are people who are steeped in the traditions or the passed-down knowledge of a community or tribe. They carry on the traditions, stories, and memories of their people. In every indigenous culture that I have experienced, people who have taken on roles as healers, cultural leaders, and spiritual teachers are referred to as Elders.

Also, an Elder can be really funny. An Elder has a twinkle in their eye; they have both the innocence of a child and the deep wisdom of the ancient. They know that magic exists and are playful with it. They know how to balance things, creating harmony and connection.

How does somebody become or be considered an Elder? An indigenous Elder will never call himself or herself an Elder. What happens is the community that they are from, the people, will recognize his/her wisdom—the fact that they are tradition bearers, healers, cultural leaders, and spiritual teachers. This is more than acknowledgment of their age; it is a term of respect for their lifetime commitment to embody, practice, and share indigenous wisdom. Through their actions, decisions, practices, and knowledge, an Elder is seen for who and what they are, are sought for their wisdom, guidance, and counsel. And, by doing so, the people, the community, give the title of Elder.

The wisdom that indigenous peoples, in particular the Elders, have is more important than ever. And this wisdom is our interconnection, our circle of life, as represented so beautifully by the sacred eagle hoop.

WHY IS THIS WISDOM NEEDED?

Look around you. Look around in your community, town, city, state, country, and the world itself. Look at our media, our politics, our businesses, our culture. You will see that people act as if they are separate, alone, and have no relations. As a result, we think and behave in ways that cause needless suffering, further division, and reckless destruction. We act as if our behavior does not impact the circle of life, and as a result of that denial, we are out of harmony.

How do we get back into harmony? Indigenous wisdom tells us that it is by living in connection with all life—with all people, the earth, and spirit. The four sacred gifts can give us the support and guidance to get there.

THE PROMISE OF THE FOUR SACRED GIFTS

The prophecy of the sacred eagle hoop is an urgent message for these urgent times. And, being an indigenous prophecy, it does not revolve around a single person, prophet, or hero. The focus of the prophecy is not on the messenger but rather on the message itself, and the collective community or tribe that holds the message. This is good news.

You and I, all of us, indigenous and non-indigenous, are meant to fulfill the message of the hoop with its four sacred gifts. The hoop prophecy does not predict the future; rather, it presents the probable positive or negative consequences of not heeding the original instructions from spirit. This is what is needed to joyfully fuel our hearts, thoughts, and actions in order to deepen our understanding, to live the truth, the reality, that we are all connected.

So if you do not remember where you came from, your culture, or your tribe, you have now found your Home. Welcome to this community, the community of human beings who accept these four gifts from the Pan-Indigenous Collective of Elders, and who will use their power to create harmony and connection with all other beings.

The time for bringing together the Medicines of the Great Hoop of Life has come. It is a time that has been prophesied by peoples all around Mother Earth for a long, long time, and so we can open our hearts to hope.

—PAT MCCABE, NAVAJO ELDER

1

The Illusion of No Relations

Through the nomadic perspective, through the spiritual perspective, through the indigenous perspective, we are part of the circle of energy that flows from the land, through the plants, through the animals, through the rocks, through the wind, and then through to mankind.

—CAROL PETTERSEN, MENANG/NGADJU ELDER OF
THE NOONGAR NATION, WESTERN AUSTRALIA

IF YOU LOOK AT all the problems—social, economical, political, environmental—that exist now in our lives, in our communities as well as around the world, we generate all sorts of reasons why these problems are occurring between human beings, between humans and nature, between humans and the earth. Things are changing so quickly, we feel and operate out of panic, out of a breathless fear.

Too often, I am tired, stressed, and overwhelmed. You may be, too. Like a swimmer against a dangerously fast current, we are left gulping and gasping for air.

Our minds, hearts, and spirits can become quickly overloaded with the magnitude of the problems, the fast pace, and the results that appear to be unsolvable. We start to shut down, despair, and suffer. A way to quiet ourselves, to stay open and not closed, is to look at our unexamined assumptions about our relationship to the world around and in us. Honestly looking at our assumptions, we can see that many of them come from a belief system that we exist only as individuals, separate and alone.

We are all susceptible to the notion of separateness, resulting in feelings of alienation and isolation from everyone and everything around us. In that "I am separate" mind-set, we can feel miserable while at the same time not take responsibility for our actions, negatively impacting others and ourselves.

An indigenous descriptor of this mind-set and this way of feeling and behaving would be: *We are acting as if we have no relations.* Everything and everyone around us is sensed as a potential threat. In this "them versus me" way of thinking there is a scary sense of being surrounded by otherness. Living inside this illusion of no relations, we feel unsafe and don't offer or ask for needed support.

What happens as we continue to operate out of this belief of isolation? We create and feed conditions that foster hopelessness, division, and even cruelty and terrorism. Through our collective and personal fear-based behaviors and actions, we lack recognition of our commonalities and shared human being—ness. For example, we fall prey to xenophobia, the fear of others, perhaps a fear of homeless people in our community. It becomes routine to turn our eyes away, even pretend they don't exist, rather than acknowledging their presence with a compassionate smile and hello.

At the same time, the "I am separate" mind-set causes us to behave toward the natural world as if we are not connected to it, as if it is something to own, use, and dominate, resulting in unlimited resource extraction, pollution of our environment, degradation of our food and water, climate change, the extinction of species, and more.

Isn't it time to wake up? Time to end the destructive illusion that we have no relations? We are hurting ourselves, we are hurting nature and the earth, and we are hurting the spirit that nourishes our world and us.

Thankfully, there is another way to live.

REAWAKENING OUR INDIGENOUS CONNECTION

In the beginning, the original indigenous peoples of each continent lived in rhythmic connection with our earth and the natural world. It was a necessity. Survival depended on seasonal foods derived out of their immediate surroundings, clean water from rivers and lakes, and shelter made from natural resources.

These first, native people understood through observation, experience, and connection to the spirit of all life not only the practical importance of needing each other but also that their very existence was one with all of nature. Every day was attuned and in accordance to the earth, the changing seasons, and the cycle of day and night. They lived with their feet firmly on the ground and in direct contact with their natural environment, rather than separated from it by concrete, climate-controlled buildings, and automobiles. These early natives learned to harmonize their senses and bodies *in* relation to nature, not *out* of nature.

If they overhunted, they saw and felt the impact. When they gathered or planted, they knew the effect of their actions. Everything was and is symbiotic. Nature has not changed, but humans' ability to be in right relation to nature has changed. To be in right relation means to live in full knowledge of, and honoring, our interdependence and interconnection to all life. There is a joy and responsibility in living in a mutually beneficial relation with the surrounding environment, living in harmony with all the interdependent parts of our natural world.

I learned the power of our connection through the meaning of the sacred pipe ceremony led by an Elder. At nineteen years old, I was a member of OYÁTE, the Lakota and Dakota term for the People, an indigenous student club at the University of Colorado Boulder. One early morning, as the other students still slept, ten of us rose early and joined a visiting Elder for a morning tobacco ceremony. Some had experienced the ceremony before, while others, like me, were awed by it for the first time.

The smoke from the sacred pipe is the symbol of holy, spiritual power—sacred winds in motion in the interconnected circle of life. The stone that makes up the bowl comes from the mineral relations. The wood that is the stem of the pipe comes from the plant relations. Both are sacred. When put together, the bowl represents the female and the stem represents the male joined in symbolic union. The sacred pipe is decorated with eagle feathers, representing all the animal and bird relations.

Lifting the pipe upward represents offering the human body to this sacred circle of life: We are all one relation on this earth. As I held the pipe for the first time, I felt my muscles, bones, my very DNA, and spirit strengthen in acknowledgment that the sacred circle holds us all. We stood in a circle as the Elder filled the pipe with tobacco and offered it to the spirit of all creation: Father, Mother, Grandmother, Grandfather, and to all the different directions—east, south, west, and north, the sky above, the earth below.

As the Colorado sun rose in shades of red, gold, and yellow, the Elder with the pipe in his hands said in a solemn voice, "Lighting this pipe, we unite all of life into one, making the oneness understood." Holding the bowl of the pipe with both hands, he pointed the stem to the sky, then he turned and pointed the stem to the east, turned again and pointed the stem to the south, then the west and the north, and finally he pointed the stem to the earth.

Next, he held the pipe before each of us in the circle. I remember closely watching him and the others. When it was my turn, I took a deep, cleansing breath, inhaling and exhaling the fresh morning air. In front of me the Elder held the red pipe bowl. Not having smoked before, I carefully touched the wooden stem and slowly inhaled, then exhaled the smoke while keenly aware of my gratitude to Father Sky and Mother Earth. I can still recall through the ritual, the loving sensation in myself and in my circle of OYÁTE friends, the reunion of all things.

The blue sky and air were now warmed by the morning sun. We remained standing in a close circle. Our Elder continued his instructions. We leaned in even closer so as not to miss a single word of his wisdom. With steady voice and twinkling eyes he continued, "The pipe is meant to remind us of our need for other human beings, the plants, the animals, the water, the minerals, the spirit, everything. Our power grows as we stand in that center of connection for our spiritual, mental, emotional, and physical growth, and our safety."

He heard my question before I even opened my mouth. "Yes, our safety, too. There will be those who teach you in the non-indigenous world that you are only individuals. But you are each a special individual who is an important part of the larger whole, of all our relations. So when you stand in the center of connection and think and act on behalf of the greater good of all our relations, you will also ultimately be of service to yourself, the individual.

"If you operate out of greed, only you matter and you forget our sacred connection, then you do not live in harmony, then destruction of other beings ultimately results in your destruction. Your safety, our safety and well-being, requires us to remember just as we do each time we hold ceremony."

This tobacco ceremony is one of the sacred traditions and practices to acknowledge the Great Mystery—an indigenous way of standing in our connection, which came from spirit and from observation of people and nature. The Great Mystery is sometimes called the Great Spirit; it is a concept of universal spiritual force.

This wisdom can help anyone in their own life to wake

up and detach from the illusion that they are separate, alone, or *not enough*. Without this wisdom, we operate as if we are fragmented and scattered; we live as if we are not needed, that we don't belong anywhere. It is from indigenous Elders that I learned, more deeply, about what it means to truly belong and be in relationship with another—human, animal, plant, or mineral—and to listen with the softest part of my ear and an open heart.

Even as I struggled as a *mestiza*—a mix of Mexican-Spanish blood and indigenous Aztec blood—I never felt questioned about my wholeness when I was in indigenous ceremonies, circles, sweats, blessings, or cleansings. Each time, my heartstring, like an umbilical cord, was made clearer and stronger between me and my mother, my grandmother, and my ancestors. With each ceremony came less struggle and deeper comfort to practice walking on this earth, bridging the powerful ordinary and powerful extraordinary worlds of earth and spirit. Even more, being present in these communities and circles, present to Elders' words, healings, and traditional knowing and wisdom, fueled my optimism and joy in being a human being, dissipating my illusion and fear that my hurts and pains defined me.

The Elders' wisdom and healing do not only belong to me: they belong to you, to all of us. Everyone has access to it because, ultimately, at the beginning, we all came from indigenous tribes, even if we have lost our story of those origins. Even if our minds have forgotten, we can take heart and reaffirm that we are part of the abundance of life, and that we are interconnected.

My uncle from the Osage reservation would draw a circle in the air while saying, "To live as a whole human being is to live in balance, understanding our connection to people, to earth, and to spirit; to hurt one of these is to hurt all of these; to love one of these is to love all of these." This gave me a clear picture of what is true abundance: the intimate interconnection of all life, and that I receive and give back to this life.

I understood his words to mean that when I treat you with dignity, when I treat you with care, whether at home, in the workplace, or in my community, I am not only showing dignity to you but I am showing dignity to people, earth, and spirit. I remember as a little girl listening to him and thinking: *Wow, I have a lot of power!* It's amazing how easy it is to grow up thinking that you do not have that power. You begin to lose sight of what is real, what it really means to be a whole human being, and what it means to have this original wisdom.

The reemergence of the felt experience of belonging in the larger consciousness (our collective interdependence and evolution), not only in our own lives but also in our connection to all things, requires action from all of us, you and me. Such action embodies the wisdom that is held in the practices of indigenous cultures and illustrates what is missing in the modern world, which are represented by what the four sacred gifts offer: the action to forgive the unforgivable, the action to heal, the action to unite, and the action to hope. These four indigenous gifts, these four sacred actions, were given by the indigenous Elders from around the world to help you and me find the way through problems, fears, and suffering and to live in true peace and harmony.

Now, more than ever, we need to be curious and examine our own mind-set and listen to spirit, to the earth, and to wise Elders from all the different directions, from all the different ages and parts of the world. Listen to the Elders, who generally share an optimism that life's problems can be solved, and who embody calmness in facing difficult situations and tough decisions.

Listen to our Elders, who hold the understanding that every thought and action has an impact that either lends support to or destroys our interconnected life and community. The voices of many wise ones share in the message that the honor of one is the honor of all; the hurt of one is the hurt of all.

To embody the indigenous wisdom of our interconnection does not mean there are no longer any difficulties, that you have achieved enlightenment and will not face challenges. Difficulties will still happen. Joy will happen, so will hardship, but there is a spirit, a wisdom that informs both the ordinary and the extraordinary. This wisdom is necessary for humanity to move forward and evolve.

Intelligence or knowledge alone is insufficient. Indigenous wisdom is foundational; it is an ability to sense the truth of life at the macro and micro levels. It is a living wisdom that expands and grows with further development as generation after generation tests its truth in the context of today.

As Chief Oren Lyons has often said: "Our leaders must never take away the hope of the people, their trust that, when we live as whole human beings, we are caring for each other, Mother Earth, and all beings, when we don't do this then we all suffer."[1] Ultimately, what I have come to understand from Chief Oren Lyons, and from other Elders, is that the indigenous wisdom is more important now than ever, so that we can respond to life's desire to renew itself rather than destroying each other, our climate, our ability to provide for future generations, our own species, and the offspring of other species.

When we understand that we are all connected, then it is difficult to be stingy with our love and care for others, because we are all part of that abundance. In living the balance of our connection to people, earth, and spirit, life will renew and renew and renew. The power to create happiness and joy is in each of us. It is individually ours and it is ours collectively.

As part of an indigenous worldview, the circle of life—the reality of our profound relatedness—contains more power than we realize to support life . . . *and* to destroy life. Therefore, we each have a choice of what we create in our hearts, in our minds, and in our communities to support our life-giving connections on earth and for those around us.

What will be your choice?

2

Receiving the
Four Sacred Gifts

IT IS THE END of winter in 1995, a warm and beautiful day for the annual American Indian Science and Engineering Society's Leadership Summit, which provides training to hundreds of inquisitive high school and college students from dozens of different Native American tribes and indigenous people from North America.

It is an annual highlight for me to attend and be with friends and Elders, and to volunteer my time to present workshops, providing skill development for the students. Ironically, I am there to teach the students personal and leadership development and diversity skills. I have been a consultant, teaching for nineteen years, in corporations and nonprofit organizations comprised primarily of non-indigenous people. The topics I teach include communication, conflict management, working with differences, and how to keep your cultural values in places that may hold practices and beliefs that are antithetical to indigenous beliefs and practices.

At forty-one years old, I come to that year's conference depleted and desperate to find the answers to my "big" life questions. I am losing hope that the executives of global corporations I have been working with can create the support to lead with a broader agenda than only the accumulation of wealth, making more and more money for stockholders without regard to the care of our earth and of the people who work for them: women and men of different races and cultures, gay, transgender, young, and old. The change is not happening fast enough; the mind-set is pretty status quo and primarily focused on stockholder value. There are so few women and people of color in upper management and executive roles. The internal work required by leaders to look at their vision, values, and behavior regarding race, gender, and sexual orientation is difficult.

Even the wonderful white men who make deep relationships across difference and can see the results to productivity and innovation ask me in confidence to remind them why they are taking this harder path in being champions of diversity. After thousands of workshops and trainings, and hundreds of coaching sessions, I am beginning to doubt my vision of creating "bridges of understanding" between people's similarities and differences around the world.

I feel like a failure in creating a mass of leaders, a movement of people who can understand that we are all one. Each time there seems to be some progress in building effective diverse communities in business, the leadership changes and we have to start at the beginning again, tackling racism, sexism, classism, and prove the power of community from scratch—again. So it is a huge relief to be here near my Elders, who can share their wisdom and guidance.

During the breaks between my workshops, I track down each one of my indigenous Elders—Dr. Henrietta Mann, Phil Lane Sr., Eddie Bent Box Sr., and others. I ask each of them the same questions: "What should I be doing with my life? What is my purpose? I want to bring healing to the world, but I'm not effective enough. I just know something is missing."

Gazing at me with her strong, beautiful, and loving face, Henrietta says, "Anita, why would I tell you something that you already know?"

As with Henrietta, all my Elders whom I urgently question listen attentively with their heads and hearts, but do not tell me an answer. However, that will all change on the second night of the conference—a special ceremony when our Elders will present some very meaningful gifts.

The next night, upon passing through the tall wooden doors of the community room, I smell the fragrant sage and sweet grass mingling in my senses. A young Indian woman smudges me with sage, cleansing me before I receive the gifts. My eyes become moist with tears as I smile, sensing a letting go of my old, heavy emotions. I am now filled with peace and expectancy. I feel fully alive and present for the first time in a long time.

There are hundreds of indigenous youth, Elders, and indigenous and non-indigenous trainers along with a few corporate sponsors gathering and sitting in concentric circles. Once seated, my whole body is transfixed on the center of our circle.

In a place of honor, I see a beautiful round wooden hoop hanging from a stand. It is made of a willow branch with dozens of eagle feathers hanging from it. The feathers look majestic, representing sacred spirit. I glance briefly at the rest of the people, and I see that this hoop is the center of our total attention as we sit quietly waiting.

As we sit silently meditating on this beautiful hoop, the Mohican Elder and keeper of the hoop, Don Coyhis, walks over to stand by the hoop and begins to speak. He tells us about a prophecy that foretold of a time when the Elders and the healers would be called to gather from the four different directions— the north, the east, the south, and the west.

He says, "Remember our Grandmother and Grandfather, Creator of All, makes no mistakes, giving life to people of different races from the different directions here on our Mother Earth. Each of us, human beings and other species, has a role to play, and all are part of the earth. The time has come as a prophecy foretold. We have been living in a great winter, and the wintertime is not over." You can hear gentle sighs of regret and acknowledgment fill the room. We are all very aware that we are still in a great winter.

"It is time to begin preparing for the spring. We cannot say if the spring is next month, next year, twenty, or a hundred years from now, but we do know that each of us, individually and collectively, has a role to play.

"When we, the Elders, gathered six months ago to prepare for this time, there was no divide between tribes. There was no fighting. There was only peace and collective action. We spoke our languages, prayed our prayers, meditated in silence, and chanted as we danced. Together we built this hoop out of a willow branch, and we tied one hundred eagle feathers onto it. Then we placed four gifts in the sacred hoop, one from each of the directions."

The silence in the ballroom, our conference community room, is full and rich. In community, we can deeply feel the importance of the Elders' gifts. We all know that spring is coming, that life and joy are rising, even in the midst of facts to the contrary. I can feel the importance of our circle of diversity, young and old, female and male, full indigenous blood, *mestizo* (mixed blood), and non-indigenous people.

One by one, Don Coyhis names each of the sacred gifts:

1. The power to forgive the unforgivable
2. The power of unity
3. The power of healing
4. The power of hope

He stops talking and slowly gazes around the ballroom. As his gaze briefly meets mine, I am filled with the seriousness of these four sacred gifts—with a joy and sense of responsibility to understand and use them fully as a human being connected to all life, people, earth, and spirit.

With our hearts and minds wide-open, I sense that there is an understanding that life itself depends upon our collective use of these gifts. Yes, the gifts are not solely for our individual or even our tribal use, but these gifts are given to all humanity to ensure that there is to be a great springtime.

The magical ceremony comes to a close, and hundreds of us

in solemn silence begin to walk out of this community room. As I step out of the room, I see two of my Elders, Henrietta Mann and Phil Lane Sr., at the other end of the hallway.

I walk over to them and ask, "I still do not have all the answers to my question, do I?"

Henrietta smiles gently and says, "Anita, you think that the worst thing that has ever happened to our people was to have been murdered and to have had our sacred lands taken? You are wrong. The worst thing that can happen to our people, or to any people, is to lose hope."

As she speaks, a sword of truth goes through my heart. I was losing hope. Now that I know my path, I have to choose to use the gifts. I have to choose to create a world that I, even as a little girl, knew was possible.

It is absolutely stunning to begin to grasp that a Pan-Indigenous Collective of Elders from the four directions, different parts of the world, gave you and me these four sacred gifts.

Initially, receiving the gifts, you may feel like it's a huge honor and responsibility for one person. As an individual, it not only feels like a serious responsibility but also feels appealing, for we each want to be special, we each want to be recognized for our uniqueness, beauty, and sacredness.

However, these gifts were never meant only for the individual: these gifts were put into the sacred hoop that holds, boundary-less, the unity of all life. You and I are a part of, not separate from, the other people, the earth and all its animate and inanimate elements, and spirit.

To believe and behave as if we are separate is not real, even though there are many messages from society that try to convince us of this lie. On the contrary, the truth is that we collectively have a lot of power and responsibility. We are the ones who get to hold the paradox of being both individual and being intimately part of this interconnected whole called life. The indigenous wisdom that all is one, all my precious relations, means that we have lots of work to do, and we have lots of joy to experience being connected to all.

How do we take this knowledge and these gifts in, integrate them, and express them in our lives? The four gifts that were given at the ceremony were meant to be healing medicine, support, and help, guiding each of us to live more fully as a whole human being, because it is not always easy to live that connection and original knowledge in our modern times.

Using the gifts initiates a cycle of spiritual evolution and practical development in being a human being. It leads to deeper understanding and, ultimately, to a knowing of our intimately interwoven relationship to everything. We yearn for wisdom, not more information. I believe the true human desire is not for more information but instead to reconnect with the original wisdom, that all of life is sacred in a precious state of relatedness.

We have the capacity and the opportunity, by virtue of simply being alive, to be conscious men and conscious women, aware that we are a precious part of a larger whole. We can *choose* to become aware, awake, and curious, to act as participants in the development of ourselves and in support of the harmonious development of our communities.

The four gifts—the power to forgive the unforgivable, the power of unity, the power of healing, and the power of hope—are yours already. The invitation from the Elders is always there for you to open. The gifts exist within each person and all around us; they are always ready for you to receive them. Simply begin, wherever you are and whenever you are called. Come join your relations and be a life-giving connection to others.

It is our duty as people to pull together to strengthen our communities, because *Motho Ke Motho Ka Batho*, a person is a person through other persons; and I am because you are.

—CONSTANCE SELOI BOND, GRANDMOTHER,
MOCHUDI, BOTSWANA

MEDICINE TO RECLAIM ALL YOUR RELATIONS

When I spoke to Don Coyhis, keeper of the hoop, during my writing of this book, we spoke about the power of "medicine" as the indigenous people and Elders see it. When the Pan-Indigenous Collective of Elders blessed and added the four sacred gifts into the hoop, they prayed their healing medicines into the hoop as well. These medicines, along with the four gifts, which are medicine themselves, recognize and bring alignment to our spiritual, emotional, mental, and physical elements, making us whole again. This medicine does not separate you into parts and categories; rather, it takes all of you as one being, all equally important and necessary to live and thrive.

So taking this definition of indigenous medicine, a way to heal and reclaim all your relations, is by reawakening your connection to nature, to people, and to the spirit of this home called Mother Earth. These heart connections are already inside of you and just need to be freed with some guidance. Here is a visualization to tap into your heart connections:

To begin, find a quiet spot (eventually you can do this in the noisiest surroundings).

First, take three cleansing breaths: Inhale through your nose and exhale from your mouth slightly open. With each breath you can feel the oxygen filling your lungs and heart.

Now imagine placing within your heart someone or something that fills you with joy, love, awe, and gratitude. It might be a baby giggling, a loved one, an adored pet or a beautiful wild animal, a stunning vista of the sea, the plains, or mountains, an exquisite flower, or a glittering expanse of stars. Whatever it is, let that presence continue to fill you, embrace you, and feed your spirit.

Stay with this image and these sensations for at least thirty seconds. With practice you can hold this image for minutes, hours, days, or longer.

As you imagine this person, loved one, or thing of nature, you may sense an opening or expansion of your heart, a feeling of joy and harmony that warms your spirit. That is your heart connection. It is your birthright, joy, and responsibility, and it is time to live it.

When you feel your heart connection deepen with practice,

you can then add another quality to this meditation. When you stay with the image and feelings of love and harmony, you can begin to visualize and connect to others.

Expand the circle of joy to include family, friends, pets, and all those you are close to. Breathe in and out as the circle expands and holds these beings.

And then after some more practice, and you feel ready, you can begin to further expand your circle during meditation to include people and beings that you don't know, and eventually to others you may find disagreeable. The intent is to recognize our oneness that we are all in relation to one another and deserving of love and respect. When you deepen your connection to others—people, earth, and spirit—you can experience this joy every day.

3

The First Sacred Gift:
The Power to Forgive
the Unforgivable

The world is in turmoil and people wonder what they should do, since it seems like the problems are daunting and overwhelming. What the indigenous Elders say is that we must change our consciousness now, shifting from the mind to the heart.

—ILARION MERCULIEFF,
UNANGAN TRIBE

IT IS A HOT, humid midsummer afternoon in 1967. My mom, younger brother, sister, and I are in the kitchen having a tall glass of ice-cold Kool-Aid. There is a knock on the door, and as always, I follow my mom to see who it is.

There stand two police officers. I am frightened to see them because they generally show up in our neighborhood to arrest someone. While watching television, I see them fire their guns at black people and other protesters.

One officer asks my mom, "Are you Mrs. Sanchez, the wife of Philip Sanchez?"

"Yes."

"Ma'am, may we come in?"

My mom opens the door, leading them into the living room.

The policeman pauses, then says, "I'm very sorry to tell you that your husband was in an accident, and he was killed at the scene."

I stand there dazed. I feel my mom as she leans heavily on me, but after a moment she somehow recovers.

The officers ask if they can sit down and ask a few more questions.

"Mrs. Sanchez, do you know of anyone who would want to hurt your husband—anyone who would want him dead?"

"No. What happened?"

"Mrs. Sanchez, it appears earlier today a white man and a black man had a heated argument in the bar around the corner from here. Your husband entered this bar several hours later and sat on the stool where earlier the black man had sat while arguing with the white patron.

"It appears the white man returned to the bar, saw your husband's dark skin, and fired two shots. Your husband was pronounced dead at the scene."

I am thirteen years old when my father is murdered, and the effects of this devastating news are a violent shock that everyone experiences throughout our family and community. We are constantly surrounded by family, aunts, and uncles who give us hugs; my mom hugs us at night before going to bed. I remember needing these hugs desperately. Mom is filled with her own grief, yet she immediately goes into action, making arrangements for my dad's funeral and dealing with all the funeral-related activities of our giant extended family.

A few days after the funeral, there is a knock at the door. We assume it will be more family members and neighbors bringing food and words of condolence. Mom unlocks the screen door with me following behind her. I peek around Mom's round body and see a slender white woman and a young boy about my age standing on our small wood porch.

The woman introduces herself as the wife and the young boy as the son of the man who murdered my father. She continues, "I am sorry to bother you, Mrs. Sanchez, but I just had to tell you that my husband is a good man. He would never have killed your husband if he knew that he was Mexican. My husband thought he was black."

The woman continues to speak, but I cannot clearly hear her words. She is saying something about black people always causing trouble. Pressing against my mom, I can feel her body tense and tremble.

My mother's stern voice interrupts the woman: "Stop! Stop! You do not even know what you are saying! You do not even know the kind of hatred you are speaking in front of your son.

I want you to know that I will try very hard to pray for you, but now please get off my porch!"

Mom closes the screen door and locks it. She walks back to the kitchen, and I can tell that she is quietly crying.

Later that evening, Mom calls all six of us children, my brothers and sisters and me, into our tiny living room. As we sit on the couch and floor, she points to the newspaper clipping with a photo of my father's body in a pool of blood.

"I want you kids to know that a white man murdered your father, not the white race. It was one man. The picture you see here in the paper is ugly and disrespectful. The dead and their souls should always be treated with respect. What you see in this paper is racism. The dead person's family, you and me, also deserve respect."

Still pointing at the photo in the newspaper, she says, "This is racism. When a violent death or an accident happens to a white person, the body is not shown, but when a black person, Indian, or Mexican is killed, the pictures are right on the front page. I do not want you to hate white people; however, you must watch where you are always, for there are ignorant people who may want to harm you.

"I believe that most people are not this way. Most people want to be kind, just as I taught you to be." My brothers, sisters, and I all sit quietly with tears in our eyes, taking in what our mother has just said.

Twenty-three years later, I receive my PhD in organization development and am now consulting to leaders of global corporations in diversity and inclusion, helping them to build strong and healthy relationships and work effectively across their different race, gender, and cultural backgrounds. During this time I begin having a recurring dream of my father's death and the visit by the wife and son of the man who murdered my father.

These dreams are vivid and in full color, except for the blurry face of the young teen boy. In my dream, his face, which is no more than a couple of feet away from mine as he stands near his mom on our front porch, has no eyes, no nose, and no mouth. It is very unsettling.

This dream continues over many months as I travel to various cities around the country, facilitating diversity workshops and building effective cross-cultural teams. Over time my dreams slowly change, and I begin to see in detail the young boy's face.

I come to understand something that the young thirteen-year-old Anita could not even imagine: I "othered" that boy to the diminishment of his personhood and individuality. I took away that young white boy's humanity, taking away his face and judging him through the actions of his father, who so violently took my father's life, and the words of his mother, who hatefully spoke of the worth of a Mexican's life over a black man's life.

As a young girl growing up in Kansas City, I had many experiences of seeing black and brown people being harmed and discriminated against in stores, in restaurants, and on the streets. I believed this young white boy's only path was to grow up with hate and murder in his heart, repeating his parents' acts of racism.

However, in rooms at AT&T, DuPont, and Hewlett Packard, my colleagues and I are facilitating retreats focused on relationships across race, women and men working together as colleagues, the challenges for women at work, and white men as change agents. We are using the community-building change process of the "talking circle": a place of belonging, trust, and safety. Modeled on indigenous practice, in talking circles only one person speaks at a time and silence is allowed. Each person has the opportunity to speak and all the other members listen with dignity and respect, without judgment.

The purpose of the talking circles is to create a safe environment for people to speak from their heart, sharing their very personal point of view and experiences with others. They gain a sense of trust in each other, discovering that what they say will be listened to and accepted without criticism. We are each bearing witness to each other, allowing both the speaker and the listeners to become positively changed on multiple levels—spiritual, emotional, mental, and physical.

During months of facilitating and listening to the stories of adult white men and women sharing how their parents had had deeply racist attitudes and attempted to instill similar prejudices in them, I learned they had chosen different paths and different beliefs as adults. I will never forget the participants' demonstrations of the courage it took to not stay silent, to actually be a leader for themselves and those they impacted around them.

Over and over, I witnessed their bravery in speaking out about forgiveness in the midst of looking squarely at the ill treatment of women and men, people of color, and other minorities in their workplaces and communities around the world. And, like dry soil that absorbs moisture, my consciousness shifted: my heart was watered by the sincerity and genuineness of these women and men who openly spoke their stories and their dreams for connection across race.

I witnessed their courage and determination to live a more compassionate future, and I was now able to let go of my deep-seated, long-held, limiting belief that true racial peace was impossible. By integrating the use of the talking circles and other indigenous knowledge into modern life, I now know that it is possible for us together to create a just world: communities and workplaces where everyone is cared for and treated with dignity and respect. I believe our individual and collective actions can consciously create racial peace; I have witnessed this coming together of different races of people who now see each other as part of their community, their family. From college campuses to the 2016 gathering at Standing Rock, North Dakota, from the Amazon rain forest to corporate boardrooms, there are people, indigenous and non-indigenous, who are gathering to be protectors of all people, earth, and spirit.

I don't know if I will ever meet the son of the man who murdered my father, but I would want him to know that I am sorry that he had to grow up knowing that his father was a murderer. I lost my father that summer day, and so did he. Today, if he appeared on my porch, instead of having him stay outside, I would invite him in.

FORGIVING MY UNFORGIVABLE

Ah, if only that was the only forgiving that I had to work on, giving that young boy back his humanity and allowing for the possibility that he may end this cycle of racism. However, my personal need for the gift of forgiving the unforgivable goes even further.

In addition to the race-based murder of my father when he was at the young age of forty-one, my father's death and its impact on me was complicated even more by the secret wish I carried in my heart—for my dad to leave our family or even to die. From the age of four to thirteen, my father sexually abused me. It ended only with his murder, leaving me filled with raw, unprocessed emotions: hurt, shame, betrayal, anger, and more.

During the days leading up to and after my dad's funeral, I allowed myself to show one part of me, only part of my truth. I would act and say, "Oh, how I loved Dad, being together with my brothers and sisters in the park playing softball, enjoying the warm breeze at family picnics under the huge Missouri oak trees. Being together cheering at basketball games that he helped to coach at the Catholic Youth Organization, listening to the music at the dances that he chaperoned." Or another story would be "I loved the laughter and dancing in our home when the calypso music came on and Dad accompanied it with his bongos. And how I loved all us six kids, my mom and dad squeezing into our old Plymouth as he drove us out of the city to visit our special Osage relatives and friends who taught us about wisdom that I did not get in school."

From the outside, I appeared to be the properly mourning thirteen-year-old who just lost her father. However, there were powerful, dark memories that plagued me. Memories of my father's hand grabbing me from behind and my little body trapped between the cold stone wall and his 230-pound body; how his hand would cover my mouth as he took what he wanted. Or when I wasn't paying attention and found myself alone in the house when he returned from work, smothering me with a pillow and his body. The horrible images played in my head: pictures of myself from age four to thirteen enduring the pain of being fondled and raped. Eventually, I gave up fighting off my father and accepted the shame of staying silent.

Now, with my father dead, I asked myself, *Did I have a part in killing Dad? Will all these memories of violence ever go away? Was my dad's death a blessing or a curse? Do I tell my family about the abuse? Will my family be okay?*

To be the target of racism and sexism/sexual violence is intensely personal. In response to my trauma, I built a shield of protection around myself. This imaginary body of armor did keep out some bad stuff, but with time I realized that it also imprisoned me. Walking around with this imaginary body armor was heavy lifting and took lots of energy, and its weight caused me to feel like I could only take shallow breaths from the chest up. The rest of my body was starving for life-giving oxygen. It became painfully clear that my armor kept out the good stuff as well. I called this body armor my "illusion-of-separateness armor." This separateness was slowly killing me, removing me from the life-giving connections and the beauty within and around me.

It turned out that once I found myself in a caring, supportive community, I could begin to imagine letting go of that heavy armor. In my journey to forgive the unforgivable, I chose at eighteen to leave my home and large family in Kansas City and go study at the University of Colorado in Boulder. It was there that I developed rich, fulfilling relationships with various people in the student organizations OYÁTE (a Native American students' group) and UMAS (United Mexican American Students).

It didn't take long being in this fertile ground that I felt stronger, as if I could feel the oxygen clear down to my toes at times. Identified as a potential leader by members of these and other student communities, I took the risk of being seen, using my voice, and stepping into leadership roles. Standing in my well of pain and my well of joy, I was elected as the first Latina and Native American student body tri-president, serving in this role from the spring of 1974 to the spring of 1975.

At the same time, I began to learn more about the rich history, traditions, and practices I have as an indigenous person and as a Mexican-American. And I dare not forget there were also many white men and women professors, administrators, and students who I opened up to. They, too, became true friends, truth-tellers, and allies. I could see the happiness, strength, and brilliance in them, and they saw the same in me. In this rich soil and mountains, originally walked by the People of the Arapahoe and Ute tribes in Colorado, I began to quench my thirst for the water that comes from being in sacred community and healthy connection with others. With every step I took, my armor slowly dropped off; it was replaced with new learning and trust in these new relationships, in myself and in my ability to speak of my pain, no longer choosing to stay silent about the violence inflicted on me as a young girl.

I regularly became part of talking circles, healing ceremonies, and sweats, attending powwows as well as Mexican fiestas and marches for peace. This new home was like an oasis, for the Elders were regular visitors to the campus. I took every opportunity to go sit and listen to them. I now understood why my mom, with no spare time, would find ways to be in service to others. I began volunteering my time to give back to the community in service.

It was here, as well, that I expanded my trust of nature to include the powerful foothills and Rocky Mountains. During these years at the university, my mother would laugh as I continually asked her in phone conversations to share more and more of my grandmother's Aztec indigenous practices that honored our connection to the earth.

With each daily practice, I became stronger. I also became more aware of the betrayal and injustice of how I was sexually and psychologically abused, imprisoned as a young child. It was unbearable to hold this pain right next to this newfound, deepening respect and love of others and myself, and my feeling of deserving to be loved and protected by my parents.

The contradiction of my treatment as an innocent child was excruciating, and one day, suddenly, this awareness caused me to throw some clothes into my small yellow suitcase and say to my partner (and future husband) Kit, "I have to drive home to

Kansas City right now. My father is dead; however, I have to talk to my mother. I don't know what is going to happen. I'll be back." With tears in my eyes and a box of Kleenex on the seat beside me, I drove the 640 miles to return home. In those nine hours many scenes replayed in my head. With strength of spirit I allowed myself to remember the most shameful moments of my young life . . .

The humid heat of a Missouri summer can take the energy out of even a nine-year-old. I am lying on our worn green couch reading, very still so as not to sweat even more. My father is sitting and reading the newspaper in his easy chair across the room. I realize how quiet it's become, when I hear his quiet hissing: "Psst. Psst." I try to ignore his sound by placing my attention deeper into the book, but when I glance upward away from the serenity of my book, Dad is gesturing to me with his lips pursed. I know without him saying a word that he is asking me to let him look at my private parts, to reveal what is under my cotton red shorts.

By this time I feel powerless not to obey, for over the years I have learned that in the end, if I don't, my dad always violently takes what he wants. I no longer fight off his lust and rapes; instead I silently obey. I take my small hand and put it between my legs, pulling away my red shorts and white underpants. I feel the air touching my private parts. I can't look at Dad, but I know without a doubt that I will never be free.

Suddenly, I feel the slap of a leather belt against my legs. I let go of my pants and jump from the couch. My mother is yelling at me, striking me with the black belt, repeatedly screaming, "What are you doing? You are in trouble!" I am terrified, never seeing her wild like this. Her face and the pain of the belt are too much and I try to escape, running across the living room and then scrambling up the stairs on my hands and knees as the belt and my mother's cries penetrate my heart and break my skin. She shouts, "You are bad. I will take you to the bishop, to the priests!" Trying to escape my mother, I use my hands and arms to protect my face as the belt cracks all over me and the pounding in my head grows painful.

Suddenly I shout back at my mother, "Okay, take me to the bishop! Beat me with the belt!" With a challenging voice that I have never dared use, I shout at her, "Are you going to take Dad to the bishop? Are you going to beat him with his belt? Go ahead and beat me, but beat him, too!" Tears roll down my face. The pain of the belt on my bare legs and arms are no longer as painful as Mom's shocked, angry, and disgusted look and words.

I grabbed more Kleenex as I continued to drive closer to Kansas City. Remembering this experience from twelve years ago, I could still feel a sense of shame rise up in me for yelling back at my mom and for giving in to my dad's sickness. I remembered my nine-year-old self sitting on the floor, sobbing and seeing the welts grow across every part of my body, less on my face and neck, as I dabbed the bloody spots off my legs, arms, buttocks, and chest. I felt disgusted with myself. I didn't matter to anyone.

As I completed my drive I am aware of two beliefs that I

created that day when I was nine. My first negative belief was that I am unworthy of love and trust, followed immediately by my second negative belief, that I would never be free.

I park in front of the home that I grew up in, the house that held the loving memories of my brothers and sisters, the rose bushes that I tended with my mom, as well as the horrific memories of my rape, silence, and imprisonment. I step on the old wooden porch and enter the house that seems so small now; my mother is alone, sitting and reading a book. She looks up at me, our large eyes meet, and she says, "Come tell me what is wrong."

It is like a fire hose; the questions, pain, and hurt come pouring out: "Mom, where were you, all those years, why didn't you protect me?" At one point I am so filled with emotion, I think I will burst. Instead, I grab a plate off the side table and throw it on the floor, breaking it into pieces. My mom and I stare at it. Then our eyes reconnect. I sit down on the small green couch next to her, exhausted from the flood of emotions and the relief of speaking my truth.

My mom, wiping tears from her face, looks at me and says, "You are right, *hija* [daughter], I was not there for you. I can tell you, I didn't know about the rapes and the extent of the violence. I am so sorry. I prayed that your dad would stop drinking and stop his violent rages. When he was murdered, it crossed my mind that I was also responsible for his death. But that's for another discussion. What is important is *you*! Anita, I am here for you now. I will give you what you need, what you deserve, *hija*."

In that moment, I reject the illusion of separateness and

let my self-protective armor drop off of my body. From all the healthy relationships and immersion into indigenous traditions at the university, I am standing in the strength of my powerful vulnerability. I choose to trust and use the gift and the power to forgive the unforgivable.

It would take years to build a new relationship with my mother, to see her with compassion and understand that she did the best she could, with the skills she had at the time, to raise six children and be the wife of my father. The forgiveness that would grow between my mother and me would lead to open conversations about forgiveness with my sisters and brothers, and aunts and uncles—no more secrets. No more silence.

The power to forgive the unforgivable has led me to reconcile and reintegrate a new relationship to my deceased father. Today I have compassion and sadness for my father, who experienced his own traumas, and whose life was cut short by racial hatred. I don't condone his violence, and I don't know if he would have ever reconciled himself with the wrongs he committed in his life, but I have discovered that every one of us can make the choice to forgive the unforgivable.

WHY FORGIVE?

Before we embark on how we can forgive, we have to answer for ourselves: *Why* should *I forgive?* One might say it is the natural order of things to find forgiveness, if and when possible, as it's a necessary part of life, an essential part of fully experiencing the abundance of creation.

I am certain that this desire to forgive and to live with an open heart has had a physical impact on me, even on a cellular level: Dropping that heavy "illusion-of-separateness armor" allowed me to finally breathe as a whole being and begin the healing process. It also had a powerfully positive psychological, emotional, and spiritual impact, contributing to the ever-increasing quality of my life and even to the length of my time on this earth. Forgiveness for others and myself allowed me to open myself up to and grow loving relationships with my partner, my children, my extended family, and my dear friends. It supported me in letting go of my mistakes and my weaknesses, to move forward in good health and self-care, toward what I wanted most for others and myself.

As you learn forgiveness, you learn compassion and empathy, creating the possibility to live as a whole human being, experiencing the joys of being alive and the joys of being in connection to people, earth, and spirit. Learning forgiveness allows you to free up energy and the space in your mind and heart; it allows you to seek compassionate justice in fostering a world of caring, equity, and inclusion, not as a result of wild and wounded revenge but, ultimately, out of peace.

In my life, forgiveness gave me the clarity of mind to be present and to focus on what was really happening. I was able to discern when specific actions were appropriate, how and where to obtain harmony and equity, and how to recognize allies and real collaboration. Ultimately, by finding peace for myself, I was able to create and extend peace for those to whom I was connected. It gave me the opportunity to translate the indigenous Lakota principle of "all my relations" into how I could make sense of the deep hurts that needed healing in my world, including the very intimate tragedies that had such devastating consequences for my family and for me.

So, why should you forgive?

Because it gives you *true freedom* to help create positive change, be in love, and stay in love with others and with yourself. You learn to act from a place of empathy, rather than one filled with anger, hate, resentment, revenge, and distrust. In forgiveness, the Elders remind us, we are all one—our spirit is tied to the spirit of the other; it is fundamental to our capacity to be healthy and whole human beings.

HOW DO WE FORGIVE?

Elders from the four directions teach us from their various traditions, their medicines, that forgiveness is releasing ourselves from the prison of what did or did not happen or what we wished had or had not happened, in order to stand in the circle of life as a whole human being. Through forgiveness we stand alive and connected to what is unfolding right now.

When we choose to end or limit the suffering that we experience from any kind of hurt or mistreatment—no matter how small, no matter how great—the act of forgiving releases the pain and resentment and allows us to be more fully in the present. Of course, some things are much easier to forgive than others: small transgressions or omissions, like your family member forgetting your birthday or your anniversary or a coworker forgetting to acknowledge your contribution to a business project. Fortunately, forgiveness can happen easily in those instances.

The process of forgiveness can take much more time, courage, and commitment when the transgression is larger, or when it happens repeatedly, or to whole groups of people, or to nature. It can take months, years, and decades to forgive, and when we are locked in the righteousness of our pain and hurt, there is an insidious illusion that *these pains and hurts are my identity*. In that space, it may even seem impossible to forgive what appears to be unforgivable: abuse, atrocities, and large-scale and intergenerational trauma.

How do we forgive the unforgivable?

The Elders' voices echo in my heart: "To be a whole human being is to live in harmony and connection with all life." I understand that the joy and responsibility to live as a whole human being—the desire to be a life-giving connection with the abundance of life, people, earth, and spirit—is what creates a yearning and, ultimately, makes the ability to forgive the unforgivable more powerful than the offense(s).

Forgiveness then becomes an empowering act of spiritual alchemy, a powerful medicine transforming the hurt into a source of deeper compassion and relationship with oneself and others in the hoop of life. On my journey, it was a major shift in my heart, mind, and soul to move from this mental attitude of *I can't . . . and I am this pain* to *I choose . . . to forgive, to be free, to be happy.*

As we open ourselves to the transformative power to forgive and to the ways it can free us to experience joy, it is also helpful to remember what forgiveness is not. Contrary to what many people believe, to forgive does not mean you condone or give up your power. To forgive does not negate the wrong that was done to you or the feelings you are experiencing.

The power to forgive the unforgivable does not mean that you are lacking confidence in yourself, or in your values and principles, or in your strengths. The power to forgive the unforgivable does not mean weakness. The power to forgive the unforgivable does not mean giving up on creating justice for yourself or others who have been wronged on a small scale or on an unthinkably huge one.

The power to forgive the unforgivable does not mean pardoning or helplessly accepting an act that is horrific against human beings, other species, or nature. It does not mean no longer requiring an apology, an assurance that mistreatment will not happen again, and even some kind of reparation for the mistreatment.

Forgiving the unforgivable does not mean the avoidance of justice. It does not mean the mistreatment or the harm is forgotten. In fact, most of the acts that people think are unforgivable cannot be forgotten; they are remembered for us to learn from. Forgiveness is not about forgetting.

It is your choice to forgive or not. The power to forgive the unforgivable, like all the gifts, is inherently yours and ours collectively to receive, open, and use. Forgiveness is a powerful medicine, a process and journey to freedom and wholeness, if taken. When we choose to use this gift, to embark on this journey, what does it require of us?

There is not one answer or one way. Sometimes our empathy, or simply considering the possibility of forgiveness, moves us immediately to action. Or our surroundings and other people can support us in considering forgiving the unforgivable. At times, we may be surprised to discover that something is shifting for us on the spiritual level—that we are growing ready to step toward forgiveness.

To use your power to forgive the unforgivable, a first step is to stop running away. Running away can be an appropriate response to a dangerous location or person. When I say stop running away, I am saying stop denying that there is a hurt to be recognized. Stop constantly blaming others or things outside of yourself for your condition, or self-medicating with alcohol or drugs to avoid facing the pain. While there are many different things that can help you to stop running, all of them require you to open your heart to yourself.

You may do this through deeply connecting to children, loved ones, animals, the natural world, your own cultural traditions and ceremony, your spirituality, or your dreams and visions. Each one is a powerful path to seeing the importance of being here, in the present, and stop running. This realization of sacredness, including your own, can help you to stop, to choose to reach toward wholeness, to stand in your power to write your own story. This is part of the original instructions: to recognize your sacred connection to all things.

Once you stop running, the pain can initially feel overwhelming. However, it is an illusion that nothing exists beyond the pain of the hurt or transgression; that nothing exists beyond the abuse, racism, sexism, classism, other discrimination, or crime that has taken place. In fact, you are supported by all our relations. You are not alone.

To authentically forgive the unforgivable, I find that I must always call for support: from my Elders, loved ones, community, nature, or spirit guides (a person, animal, bird, or element that bring me safety and wisdom). To face the hurt, we need loving community with another human being, our family, our larger tribe, or all our relations in nature. We need to be grounded in the knowledge that we are worthy by virtue of being a human being. Dealing with trauma, one must acknowledge what has happened and remember that one is still worthy of love.

For me, it was a major step to stop running and face the truth that I was worthy of and able to accept love that was coming from nature, spirit, and other human beings. My thinking was: *How could anyone love someone who is so damaged?* rather than: *They love a human being who is worthy of dignity. I am amazingly strong, resilient, and beautiful.*

You may find that when you first begin to lower your body armor of protection, it is a bit scary. I find that if I do not sense a loving human community around me, then I will go and find my support elsewhere. Community with all my precious relations can be felt by sitting quietly in meditation, and in that silence we can rediscover the true sacredness of the land, people, and spirit we are part of. I have never had a tree, a rock, water, birds, or fire lie to me, so nature has always been a good place to start. The connection to nature is a spiritual path in the physical world to seeing and always remembering our life-giving connections, giving us the sense of peace, support, and courage we need to face the pain.

When you decide to truly face the hurt, your next step is to name its presence and allow yourself to experience the pain where it lives in your body. You can sit, stand, sing, or dance with the pain and really feel where it lives in you. As my Elders taught me to be in nature and observe its effect on me, I became much more attuned to what was happening in my body. I could sense the oxygen flowing and where it felt stuck.

In my early years of wearing my "illusion-of-separateness armor," I felt as if the oxygen was constricted in my neck or chest. Using my imagination and time with nature allowed me to discover what was stuck in there: unwanted trauma and pain, the spiritual scars that have an impact on my physical, emotional, and mental body. Discovering where it appeared in my body, I became conscious of how I was still carrying the trauma. Then I could focus on releasing the emotional and physical pain that was stuck in that place, freeing me to do the work of choosing to forgive.

Once you have clarity about the hurt and mistreatment, you now can ask, *What do I want to do with it?* Your choice is to let go of the hurt by forgiving the perpetrator(s) or to choose not to forgive them. If you choose not to forgive, you are choosing what may seem easy but is actually harder, for you will stay imprisoned by the past event and your suffering, choosing to carry the weight of toxic hatred and pain.

If you choose to forgive and release the pain, hurt, or mistreatment, at the moment you choose, it may simply disappear, leaving you with a sense of lightness and new energy. If it does not all dissipate, you can ask Mother Earth, Father Sky, your spirit guides, or another higher power to take the rest away. Then you are free, and you can choose what you want to fill the place where there was once only pain, suffering, or negative emotions. Some choose to put love there, green gardens, images of loved ones, or dreams and visions of what is hoped for.

What is powerful is that there is not just a letting go of pain when you forgive; there is also the opportunity to create a new, healthy love for yourself that lets go of your anger and blame. That self-love allows reintegration of a relationship with the other, releasing them from the bondage of "perpetrator" and allowing them to step into the fullness of their humanity.

In my dreams, I recognized the horror of taking away a young boy's face, a boy whom I didn't even know. It was painful to face the shame of what I had done to this boy, even though I had only been thirteen. As his face emerged from the brokenness within my inner core, it was as if a light was beginning to shine. I could no longer, as a whole human being, hold this inside of me and allow myself to disconnect from another human being. I could no longer continue to take away his face, to erase and deny his humanity. In this process, I was able to forgive myself and eventually to forgive the murderer of my father.

My work was not for me to forget what happened. Instead, my path was to use the energy freed up by forgiveness and to take it out into the world to be a life-giving connection to others.

TURNING TOWARD THE SUN

After I moved away from home, oh, how I treasured the visits from my mother and her two sisters. We would sit for hours around the table, sharing food, laughter, and inevitably, stories of my grandmother Medina. My mom, with a longing smile, would say, "Every day in growing season, Grandma would have me rise early with her to cook tortillas, beans, and eggs. She would raise her hand multiple times during the cooking, giving thanks to the spirit, to the earth, to the water, and to this food that provides nourishment for all of us."

Mom continued: "Once the sun was up, we would be in the garden. Your grandma would say, 'Look, *hija*, the flowers are turning all day long toward the sun. They are *mirasols* [sunflowers]. No matter if we are in health or sickness, no matter what is happening outside of ourselves, we must remember to look at the sun. It is a new day. Remember this, *hija*, for, in remembering, you and your brothers and sisters and our family will enjoy life.'" As I listened to their stories, I was learning even more deeply just how important this lesson is for orienting away from pain and toward life.

So when people ask me, which is often, "How do indigenous people continue to be in relationship with people, earth, and spirit after all that has been done to you: your land taken, genocide of whole tribes, displacement, and endless harassment? How can you forgive the unforgivable?," I take a breath, draw in the plant spirit of cleansing sage, and connect to the voice within me and to the voices of my mother, my grandmother, and the Elders: "Yes, our lands were taken; our people were killed in greed; our children were placed in boarding schools, suffering rape, sterilization, even death; and our spiritual traditions were made illegal.

"Our people are reeling from the effects of alcoholism, drug addiction, suicide, abuse—toxic remnants of the hurts and mistreatment. However, the miracle is that we are still here. Many of our traditions and spiritual practices remain intact.

The Elders teach us that to be a whole human being is to live with the original knowledge of our connection to all and to orient toward the springtime. We are getting stronger. Indigenous women are raising their voices, joined by men, in healing our families and communities. We are young and old, speaking for our Mother Earth in order to protect her and the life she provides for all beings.

"And, most important, as we hold in the deepest part of our hearts the knowledge that we are all connected, we are compelled to forgive. We also get to choose to use the gift of forgiving the unforgivable. We get to choose to turn toward the sun, to focus on what wholeness we want to create, to live as whole human beings who are a life-giving connection to all."

I still come back to the teachings of Chief and Elder Phil Lane Jr. of the Yankton Dakota and Chickasaw Nation. He created a powerful film entitled *Healing the Hurts*, focused on his work in helping people forgive the unforgivable: to name and free themselves from the trauma endured as children when they were forced to leave family, culture, and tradition, and live in residential schools in North America. The point of the Indian residential schools was to complete the physical and cultural genocide of many tribes by beating the Indian out of the Indian, as has happened to indigenous people in many other parts of the world, across Asia, Africa, Europe, and Australia.

I'll never forget Phil Lane Jr. saying, "Who better to teach forgiveness than the person who has been whipped?" I first thought: *This is unfair! To be the one who is abused/assaulted and then have to be the one to forgive?* In the past, I often wondered: *Who I am to speak of forgiving the unforgivable, especially when people have experienced such large-scale atroc-ities against them? Am I qualified to teach forgiveness?* Then I remember Phil Lane's words, a lesson for all of us to remember, and ponder for ourselves.

Personal trauma that is connected to the trauma of the group requires the presence of the community and its healing energy for us to become completely free. Going inward and developing that freedom with the support of a community, whether a family, a tribe, a church, or nature, benefits not only the individual but also the entire community. Simply bearing witness and carrying someone else's story strengthens the bonds of community.

Please remember, however, that forgiveness doesn't mean forgetting. It doesn't mean not seeking justice to change things or to repair what has happened. As the Elders have said, for-giveness creates the fertile ground to true freedom. And, first and foremost, one of the ultimate acts of self-love is to free oneself. One of the ultimate acts of love of all beings is to free all beings.

FORGIVENESS IS A SPIRITUAL PATH

In 2009, the eagle hoop with the four sacred gifts and its new eagle feather staff traveled across the United States. Don Coy-his, other Elders, and the indigenous communities prayed and used the power of forgiving the unforgivable to heal themselves, their families, and their communities of the genocide caused by government policies to rid the land of the Indian. The journey continues to use the medicine of forgiveness to create harmony and connection between all people, earth, and spirit.

Forgiveness is a life-affirming, conscious act of power, not weakness, because the forgiver holds and uses this power to free and heal all those involved, both victim and perpetrator, so both can become whole human beings again. This tremendous power to forgive the unforgivable is beyond letting go. It is actually a reintegration and formation of a new, healthy, and whole relationship with the self and others. The steps taken in the forgiveness process may vary, but its purpose is based not just on morals or ethics but also on the desire to not hold on to the anger and instead move forward and evolve.

Forgiveness can then be understood as a spiritual practice as taught by the Elders. We all have a choice: We can use violence, both physical and emotional, to control and exert power over someone or something, or we can choose another way. We have an opportunity to choose a way that brings harmonious development and the harmonious connection among all of us through spiritual practice, calling on our higher selves, our beliefs, and our actions in something greater.

For many indigenous people, that "something greater" is our Mother Earth, who affirms our place as part of a huge expanse of life. Taking the time to appreciate and be with nature is an important spiritual practice, opening our minds and hearts to forgive. Walking on Mother Earth, breathing in the oxygen, feeling the sunshine and the rain, you are receiving her grace and loving hug, the reassurance that we are part of something larger, that we are supported as we walk our higher spiritual path of letting go and forgiving.

After years and years of working on forgiveness, and feeling pretty good about my progress, I remember clearly one day when an East Indian colleague asked me, "Anita, have you fully forgiven your father for his abuses to you?"

Whenever a child loses a parent, it is a defining moment, especially when it happens at a young age. His death was more complicated, not only because he was murdered, but also because I had wished for his death, so I would no longer have to live in fear of his abuse. So my colleague's question of whether I had fully forgiven my father was emotionally intense and complex; it asked if I could have real compassion for my father, and not lock him into the role of a perpetrator. The question also led me to ultimately ask if I could have true compassion for myself. The only way to get there was to finally stop running away and face the trauma once again from this new place of compassion.

I was invited to look inward and face the painful memories and feelings, not run away from them. To forgive the unforgivable of what my father had done to me was the only way to find freedom from my own guilt, anger, and shame. Forgiveness was the fertile soil for true healing, reconciliation, and reintegration of myself, and of my father, too. This process was more profound and life changing than I could have ever imagined.

As I related earlier in this chapter, when I was finally able to lay down my suffocating illusion-of-separateness armor, no longer staying silent in my pain, and with the help and guidance of my indigenous Elders and community, I was able to finally dig deeply within myself and find that my soul was ready to forgive my father. When I related my whole story to my colleague, he responded, "Anita, there is still more to do. You have not fully forgiven him." I was puzzled, because I felt I had consciously and authentically used this gift, the power to forgive the unforgivable.

He said to me, "You haven't thanked your father for giving you life."

I can still feel my physical reaction when he said that. I went outside and walked among the rocks and the trees, receiving nature's help to clear my head and my heart. He was right. I still had work to do. In that moment, I chose to let go of the last ashes of anger in my heart by transforming it into gratitude. A short time later I was inspired to create a video about the four gifts and how they have transformed my life. I ended it by saying, "I thank my father and mother for giving me life." In the presence of others, in a public way, I wanted to say and feel its authentic truth. I found, in speaking it aloud, that feeling of gratitude begin to blossom in me, and it continues to grow to this day.

The power to forgive the unforgivable is a gift that you can choose to open and use.

Do I still get triggered? Do others still hurt me? Do I question, sometimes, if I want to forgive? Yes, without a doubt, I am continuing my journey. When I start to feel that way, my practice tells me I can choose to open and use this gift.

I remind myself that rage hurts the host, the victim, but rarely the perpetrator of the wrong that has been done, and I choose to honor my precious spirit. The Elders say that to be a whole human being is not easy, but once you begin on the path, it is hard to return to your old ways, because you will feel the separation from the joy that is now yours. You will be aware of the abundance you are missing.

THE FERTILE SOIL OF RECONCILIATION

When it comes to forgiving the unforgivable, we have much to learn from South Africa. Nowhere has this lesson come home for me more poignantly than in my corporate diversity and inclusion work. At one such gathering, in Virginia, we were facilitating deep immersion between executives from DuPont, AT&T, and the Digital Equipment Corporation.

We were exploring many issues around race, gender, and sexual orientation in a five-day gathering, sharing not facts and figures but deeply personal stories. They were building unprecedented relationships and connections across differences, deepening their self-awareness, understanding, and skill for leading diverse workforces. They were imagining and initiating much-needed reconciliation.

On the second day of that multicultural awareness and skill-building workshop, to the surprise of everyone, a short black man, projecting a huge, powerful, loving energy, entered the room. We all stood and began applauding as we saw that it was Bishop Desmond Tutu, Nobel Peace Prize winner, and the very man who was the chairman of the Truth and Reconciliation Commission in South Africa.

Bishop Tutu was attending another meeting in that Virginia hotel. Unbeknownst to us, one of my colleagues, Richard, had spoken with him when they crossed paths during a morning walk, explained the purpose of our meeting, and asked him if he had a moment to stop in.

The bishop spoke for seven minutes about the many black South African women and men who have lost their children, their husbands, their wives, their parents, and their families to the brutality of apartheid, and yet, through their strength and forgiveness, they have found a new relationship with each other, victims and perpetrators.

He said that the Truth and Reconciliation Commission has provided a framework, but it is the individual people who have made this reconciliation possible, turning away from the debilitating effects of rage, choosing to ask for authentic apology and connection, and focusing on the new world they want to create. They consciously choose a path of forgiveness for the health of their spirits and for the health of all in their society, grounded in their love of their beautiful land. He said that they are proving that it is possible to interrupt the feelings of hatred and to engage in forgiving the unforgivable.

In closing, he spoke about his admiration for our group's commitment to the healing process of reconciliation and his hope that the work would continue to grow. When he had finished, my colleagues and I walked out of the room with him, and Bishop Tutu said, "Richard tells me that all of you have been doing reconciliation—race, gender, sexual orientation, age, and other areas—for a very long time. This is good but not sufficient."

As he turned to leave us, he asked, with a twinkle in his eye, "What's next?" And as we shall shortly see, this is the perfect invitation to the second sacred gift: the power of unity.

As a deeply traumatized species, among many at this point, it seems we will each be faced with the opportunity to forgive the unforgivable, which has been the key to retrieve the heart and truth for me. Any and all methods, practices, for achieving forgiveness are critical at this time. The Medicine released into the world, into Life, Light and Love, that comes with authentic forgiveness, can be likened to the mirror-twin, the opposite, of an atom bomb, an exponential infusion of Grace and Light radiation into the world, penetrating all barriers, affecting every element of Creation.

—PAT MCCABE, NAVAJO ELDER

THE MEDICINE OF FORGIVENESS

Remember, medicine is anyone or anything that brings into alignment the spiritual, emotional, mental, and physical realm. The Elders are tradition bearers and healers with particular medicines to bring wholeness, and one of these medicines is the gift of the power of forgiveness.

You can approach any unforgivable that you've experienced. It could be some unforgivable personal hurt, collective trauma, or transgression against nature, people, and spirit in the world. You can prepare to use the medicine of forgiving the unforgivable by choosing to consciously and deeply invest your energy looking toward what you most want, like the flower looks toward the sun for growth and nourishment.

Close your eyes and allow a vision to arise that paints a picture or a deep feeling of the way you want your world to be in the presence of heartfelt forgiveness. You can deepen this vision if you write it down, draw it, allow images from nature to anchor your vision, and fill your heart with this new, freeing possibility.

You imagine this ideal world and allow yourself to be drawn toward it, for it to light your way forward. The vision can become so strong that it pulls you into it, transforming the unforgivable and your relationship to it. As you practice, you will find that you are supported in forgiving the unforgivable by living in that vision of the wholeness of you and all your relations.

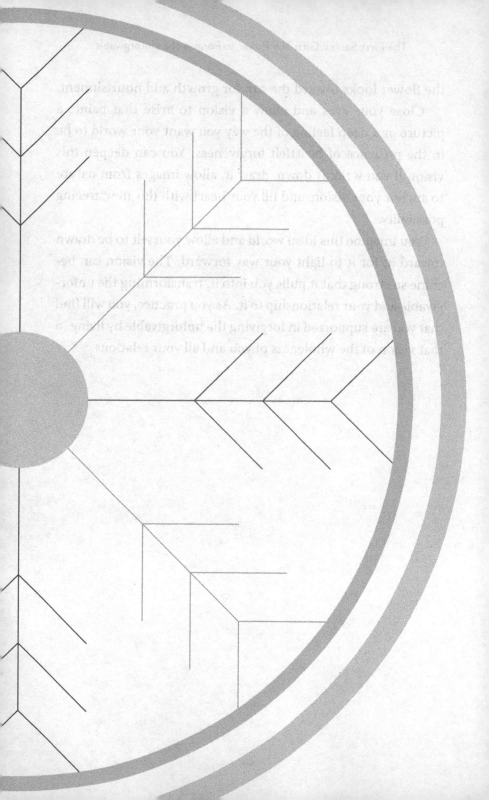

the flower looks toward the sun for growth and nourishment.
Close your eyes and allow a vision to arise that paints a
picture and a deep feeling of the way you want your world to be
in the presence of beautiful forgiveness. You can deepen this
vision if you write it down, draw it, allow images from art, etc.
to assist your vision and fill your heart with this interesting
prospective.

As you imagine this ideal world and allow yourself to be drawn
toward it, let it be light your way forward. The vision can become so strong that it pulls you into it, transforming the cater-
pillar and your relationship to it. As you practice, you will find
that you are supported in forgiving the unforgivable by living in
that vision of the wholeness of you and all your relations.

4

The Second Sacred Gift:
The Power of Unity

Sawubona says we see you and the response is Yabo Sawubona; yes, we see you, too. . . . When two human beings meet in this gesture of Sawubona, the acknowledgment is we see each other. That becomes an agreement, because we are obligated from that point to affirm the reality that seeing has empowered us to investigate our mutual potential for life.

—ORLAND BISHOP, ELDER,
CARRIER OF ZULU TRADITION OF
SOUTH AND WEST AFRICA

THE SACRED HOOP WITH one hundred eagle feathers, a medicine wheel of the four directions, is a visual depiction of the universe, our earth, and our inner universe. The Elders recognize four as the symbol of completion. From the Cherokee legend recounted by spiritual leader Lee Brown:

At the beginning of this cycle of time, long ago, the Great Spirit made an appearance and gathered the peoples of this earth together, and said to the human beings, "I'm going to send you to four directions, and over time I'm going to change you to four colors, but I'm going to give you some teachings, and you will call these the Original Teachings; when you come back together with each other, you will share these so that you can live and have peace on earth, and a great civilization will come about. . . ."

And so He gave each of us a responsibility, and we call that the Guardianship. To the Indian people, the Red people, He gave the Guardianship of the Earth. . . . To the South, He gave the yellow race of people Guardianship of the Wind. . . . To the West, He gave the black race of people Guardianship of the Water. . . . To the North, He gave the white race of people Guardianship of the Fire. . . . Each of the four races went to their directions and learned their teachings . . . [but] some of the brothers and sisters had forgotten the sacredness of all things, and all the human beings were going to suffer for this. . . . The elders knew peace would not come on the earth until the circle of humanity is complete; until all the four colors sat in the circle and shared their teachings—then peace would come on earth.[2]

Most, if not all, indigenous peoples share ancient traditions that acknowledge our unity as human beings and our unity with the earth. These core beliefs are central to walking the spiritual path with our practical feet as human beings. There is perhaps no better place, then, to witness the indigenous people of the Americas, who live in unity and honor the seasonal cycles of Mother Earth and the universal system.

In early 2016 an unprecedented gathering occurred in Standing Rock, North Dakota, in fulfillment of the "Original Teachings" given to us by the Great Spirit to protect the earth, water, and people. This movement that awakened all of us, indigenous and non-indigenous, to our relationship with the earth started with young indigenous women running relays across the land.

They started in the cold of February running across the fields, hills, and mountains of North Dakota and across the United States. The young women were compelled to run for Mother Earth in order to end the apathy—an apathy that is separating ourselves from what is happening to our Mother and each other.

With their feet hitting the ground, they began a movement that, at its infancy, was called the Rezpect Our Water campaign. The Dakota Pipeline was to run next to Bismarck, North Dakota, but the citizens of Bismarck protested their concern about the safety of the pipeline, with its possible contamination of the water and potential to decrease the value of their properties. So, without proper consultation with the Sioux Nation, the pipeline was rerouted to within one-half mile of the indigenous reservation called Standing Rock.

The women used their voices to alert the people that there would be a 1,100-mile pipeline digging into Mother Earth, which would soon be ripping through our Native peoples' burial sites and ceremonial/religious sites and harming the sacred water of the tributaries that eventually flow into the great

Missouri River, supplying drinking water to more than eleven million people.

As the young women continued to run through the spring and into the summer, their voices began being heard by more and more. In April 2016 there were just a few tents with several Elders and others who heard the call from the young women runners and from earth itself. None would have known then the magnitude of this movement: The spiritual energy called to people of all colors, ages, tribes, states, and nations to gather at Standing Rock.

Millions saw the young women runners on social media—Facebook, Twitter, YouTube—and to a lesser degree on major television stations. The women's call echoed across Mother Earth, signaling to the hundreds of indigenous tribes across Turtle Mountain (an indigenous description for North America) to heed the call. More of the Elders came, the grandmothers arrived, and the people from the tribes, who had long-standing disputes with each other, came. None of those old wounds mattered anymore.

A great healing was happening by the uniting of the tribes. The Oceti Sakowin, or the Seven Council Fires of the Great Sioux Nation, came; they had not been together on this land since 1876, at the Battle of the Little Big Horn. This is the ground where the indigenous people won the battle against Custer and the Seventh Cavalry in protecting the people and the sacred land; this is the place where our revered Chief Sitting Bull is buried. The tribes won the battle then, but they had to separate for protection, as the U.S. government prevented them from gathering again.

Since 1876, the gathering at Standing Rock is the largest historical gathering of indigenous tribes. There stands the Oceti Sakwoin camp, the Seven Council Fires; this camp is the heart of the Standing Rock gathering. It has a prominent place in a huge circle with seven tipis and in the center is a continuously burning fire. Not everybody knows the past and the present-day story of the Seven Council Fires; however, everyone, indigenous and non-indigenous, can feel the powerful presence of spirit. The sacred fire is said to be the place where there is no separation, only unity.

When you go to pray in the fire, you can look in, and the ancestors can see you, and you can sense them. Because of this, everyone is in prayer all the time. When actions are needed from us to go stand as Water Protectors in front of the corporation, state troopers, or National Guard, all the people must do this in a prayerful way, so there is no alcohol and there are no weapons. Everyone is in sacred ceremony, speaking for the earth, chanting: "Water is Life, *Mni Wiconi, Mni Wiconi.*" The young women leaders and the Elders were clear that they were not protesters but water protectors: They were at Standing Rock, asking everyone to join with peace-filled hearts to protect the sacred water.

The media messages continued to multiply, and as a result, four, five, six, seven, eight thousand began to gather in support, prayer, and ceremony with the Water Protectors. The UN sent in special observers along with Amnesty International to ensure that the peaceful Protectors of the Water's human rights would not be violated by the growing presence of police and military. This campaign that had been started by the young women relay runners became a national and eventually a growing international movement, with supporters from South America, from the Amazon rain forests, from Europe, Asia, and the South Pacific—Maori and Aboriginal tribes. Next, U.S. military veterans, native and non-native, came in the thousands, saying they were there to protect the Water Protectors. A huge ceremony was held where the veterans apologized to Native Americans for what they had done to them and asked forgiveness. The chants continued throughout the land: "Water is Life, *Mni Wiconi, Mni Wiconi.*"

On December 4, 2016, the secretary of the Army announced that the Dakota Pipeline would be rerouted. Celebration joined the fires and the prayers. Yet Water Protectors remained at Standing Rock, not knowing if, when, and where the decision will be honored, due to economic and political pressure. But the truth is that Standing Rock is a powerful victory for indigenous people; we won because of what we created with young leaders, women, men, Elders, earth, and spirit. Hundreds of tribes reunited in sacred ceremony and shared their medicine.

All who went to Standing Rock came away with healing and hope for an indigenous-centered legacy, a legacy built on the wisdom of the Elders, whose lives are steeped in prayer and ceremony, and of the young people with old spirit and women whose voices speak for her, our Mother Earth. In this new legacy, every person is important, for each is sacred and every act is sacred. Non-native and native people felt the power of kindness, visible prayer, the strength of unity on behalf of Mother Earth. Whether you were present at Standing Rock or watched on electronic screens around the world, we all felt that energy—we experienced our oneness.

As the Cherokee prophecy said, "There will come a time that we will reunite the four races, the people of the four directions, to share our original teachings from the Great Spirit, and we will remember the sacredness of all life." Another prophecy that filled the camps at Standing Rock is that these young women and young men, the youth, are the fulfillment of the Prophecy of the Seventh Generation.

The Prophecy of the Seventh Generation says that when the seventh generation of young people come, the great winter will end, for these young people with old spirits will lead and make change: A reuniting with each other and with Mother Earth will happen. They continue to run and stand in the front lines at Standing Rock, calling out in prayer, and drumming the sound of unity and our love for our Mother Earth. The young leaders united with their Elders, supporting them. They stayed on the spiritual path with their clear messages, for humans, plants, animals, fish, birds: To live we need clean water; water is sacred for us and for all future generations.

This is what the power of the Gift of Unity supports: to be in right relation, a life-giving connection with all beings. This is a time for all of us to remain united and steadfast—to protect our water, as the Water Protectors at Standing Rock are doing, and to protect our Mother Earth, repairing the world from the misuse of power and greed. This gift of the power of unity, like all the four sacred gifts, was placed into the hoop from the Elders of the four directions so that all humankind can use them. When we choose to stand in the circle of unity, there is strength. Every person, you and me, has an important part in the circle of sustaining all our precious relations: people, earth, and spirit.

THE CIRCLE OF UNITY

It is this circle of unity at Standing Rock that brings back a memory of my first day of kindergarten. I walk up the three stone steps of the redbrick building into a classroom with tall ceilings and windows. All the children look clean and shiny in their freshly pressed shorts and dresses.

The young and pretty teacher calls out our names and hands each of us a box of crayons and a piece of thick construction paper. As we sit on the smooth wood floor, she says, "Please draw a picture of what you are going to be when you grow up."

I know exactly what I want to draw. For a long time, I have this wonderful dream about what I am going to do when I grow up. Soon the floor is covered with crayons and paper, and lots of little noises fill the air as we draw our pictures.

One by one, the teacher calls our names and each of us stands in the front of the room and shows our pictures to the class. I watch as the other kids present their drawings of firemen, doctors, mommies, and teachers.

Finally, it is my turn to share my picture. It shows a large circle of the earth with lots and lots of stick people, men and women, of different colors and sizes and shapes. I say, "Look! Our hands are on each other's hearts, connecting us all around the world."

Next, I point to one of the stick figures: "This one is me. There are many of us connecting our hearts all around the world." I look out at all the faces, expecting them to be as excited as I am. Instead, there is a loud outburst of giggles.

After a pause, the teacher says, "Put away your crayons and drawings." For some reason, the children's giggles and the teacher's lack of a smile does not bother me. I know I just drew the vision of what I am going to be when I grow up.

Thinking back on my kindergarten vision, I am reminded of what Brother Chief Phil Lane Jr. said in a class: "It is an indigenous principle that there must be unity in order to have harmonious, sustainable development. Everything is connected to everything else: personal, social, cultural, and political. When we work with any one part of the circle, the whole circle is affected. Unity means oneness. If we do not have unity, then there will not be harmonious development. Indigenous Elders have taught me that the lack of this unity is the primary disease of our circle of life, the primary disease of our communities."[3]

Remember that when we live with the mind-set *I am separate,* we view the world around us as a potential threat. We act as if we have no relations and feel isolated and alone. This illusion of separateness creates an emptiness in our lives, an emptiness that lures us to find ways to fill in that gap, escape the feelings of loneliness, often through endless material consumption. This *I am separate* mind-set becomes, as Chief Lane Jr. aptly described, a "disease" to the circle of life, a disease to the human heart. Buying and having more things will never heal our loneliness.

Continuous consumption of resources without an awareness of reciprocity with the world and nature around us denies the connectedness of life. The Gift of Unity, an understanding of our connection, is necessary to begin to repair and rebalance things in a way that can bring about lasting happiness and a sustainable future for each other, our children, and the children of all species. We no longer need to try to buy our way out of feeling separate. A realization of unity can put an end to this. Be curious, ask yourself these questions: *What problem do I see happening here right now? And how am I a part of the problem? Who else can I join to help repair and resolve the problem?*

The costs of "dis-unity" are enormous: depression, crime, drugs and alcohol addiction, suicide, physical and mental abuse, destruction of the natural world, extinction of species, and a general collective despair in all communities.

What happens in China affects the United States. What happens to the rain forest causes changes in the Arctic. When one species of animal or plant becomes extinct, its effects are felt elsewhere. We are indeed interconnected, and the more we are awakened, the more we can understand the power and sensibility of this oneness. When the Gift of Unity is realized, its effects are expansive, rippling outward. When we go for a walk in a fertile healthy forest, we feel alive, stronger and healthier, and when we see a clear-cut forest, our hearts hurt and we feel the loss. In those moments we feel our intimate connection to that part of the natural world. That is an awakening.

How can we create and expand the awareness and implementation of these gifts on a global scale if people do not believe in the concept of oneness or each individual's connection to all life? There was a time when I only heard these concepts at indigenous gatherings and within some Mexican families. Times are changing.

Many different people, all over the earth, are now part of a growing movement and understanding of our unity. Global agreements are being forged to limit carbon emissions in order to stop the growing climate change. Many people from all walks of life are trying to live these principles of unity and oneness: people of all ages, all kinds of communities, including corporate businesses, who understand you cannot have sustainable, harmonious development on a battle-torn, depleted, or dead planet. For instance, the world's largest corporation, Walmart, has aspirational goals to use 100 percent renewable energy, produce zero waste, and sell only sustainable products. Sixty to ninety thousand companies that sell products to Walmart will now have to show that they are measuring and tracking their carbon footprint and beginning to reduce it.[4]

When we understand our interconnectedness, we can continue to transform the world; we can right injustices and restore the integrity of the sacred circle—people, earth, and spirit—by uniting together. We can take heart from the many movements that exist right now. There are now millions of groups around the world that are uniting together to establish equality for women, protect the rights of children, eliminate human trafficking and all forms of violence, end hunger, heal the planet, and stop global warming. We can be encouraged by this response to the suffering of the human family, the earth, and other species that is taking place as the awareness of our connectedness grows.

One of the greatest modern-day demonstrations of the power of unity is that of indigenous tribes and their allies in Ecuador, and specifically the story of the Achuar, a dream culture that lives deep in the Amazon river basin. Dream cultures have many ancient refined rituals to access dreams and integrate them into their individual and collective daily lives. Each morning, Achuar families share their dreams and, based on those dreams, decide what they will do and how they will live. They have a sense of wholeness and connection to both the invisible-spiritual and physical realms.

The Achuar Elders tell us that in the early 1990s their young and old began having dreams of a destructive force coming from the external world. Soon after, they learned that the western edge of the forest had been given over as an oil concession. Having heard of and seen past destruction, sickness, and struggles from other tribes in the northern region due to oil production, mining, and timber harvesting, the Achuar tribe began to gather together with other tribes and, struggling through many hardships, became a united voice.

Passionate, determined, and steadfast in protecting those million acres of the Amazon basin, the Achuar knew that this was their role. Recognizing that we are all connected around the world, they reached out to allies from other cultures to unite with them to protect these sacred headwaters of the Amazon, "the heart and lungs of the earth." Their partners, such as the Pachamama Alliance, the Rainforest Action Network, Amazon Watch, and members of the European community, worked with them to seek permanent protection of their lands and their culture.

They mapped the region and established clear title. They crafted culturally appropriate development strategies that ensure the vitality of the people and the forest. With their partners, they successfully blocked the large corporate interests, whose legacy of environmental destruction, pollution, and cultural displacement threatens the balance of life, community, nature, and spirit. In 2008, joining with other indigenous tribes and new government leadership, they convinced the Ecuadorian people to become the first country to declare in their constitution that nature, as an entity, had rights that must be defended. The Amazon rain forests are acknowledged to be "the lungs of our world," and the Achuar, as native inhabitants, act as stewards and protectors of this essential ecosystem.

The Achuar do not describe themselves as living *in* the rain forest. They, as a tribe, as a people, are a living *part* of the rain forest. And as long as they are able to continue to protect and live in balance with all their relations as they have for millennia, they—the fish, the birds, the trees, the waters, and all else—will be sustained and continue to regenerate.

They know this because they experience happiness and harmony with their surroundings. They know that Arutam, the spirit of the rain forest, will take care of them as long as they continue to live in accord with the unity that has always existed. As Achuar Elders explain, our collective survival is at risk, threatened by the nightmare dream of the modern world that only sees nature as an endless fount of resources without end, unaware of the destructive consequences of taking those resources.

You could say this is not our story; this is about indigenous people in Ecuador, such a long way away. Yet, as the Achuar protect their culture and fight for the rights of their environment, we can now see our relationship, our unity with them, understanding that we are all part of the same earth. When the Achuar fight to protect their culture and rain forest, their efforts directly benefit you and me, our children's future, and generations beyond. This is the gift of the circle of life, of our unity.

THE STRENGTH OF OUR UNITY

Distance, whether physical or cultural, does not need to stop us from learning from each other and naturally uniting together. A beautiful example: People all over the world are uniting to support women to combat poverty and generate new sustainable economic activity in their communities. Organizations and programs such as Grameen Bank and Kiva micro loans are emerging in all parts of the world.

Aid to women and girls for businesses, education, literacy programs, and the building of schools and hospitals is just one of the ways that reflect this coming together. These efforts, on both a local and a global level, demonstrate the positive effects this realization of our connectedness to each other can have and show the strength of our unity. We are seeing an awakening of this power and the results of using our gifts for the benefit of everyone.

At a Young Women's Christian Association (YWCA) World Council meeting I attended in Singapore, we were sitting in a circle in silence, sensing being a part of the whole, knowing that each of us had an important part to play in the lives of each other and of our world. This was our circle of unity. If so moved, we could speak to the group. At a certain point, one woman,

Mrs. Rodriguez, who had been very quiet, spoke up. She began humbly and in a soft tone, but became more and more animated as she spoke.

"I have been listening to all of you and thank you for all your efforts," she said. "I would like to recount my story in hopes that it will inspire you, as you have inspired me, to return to the circles we are part of and create a world that works for all of us."

As she spoke, she transported this group of women away from Singapore and back to her difficult life in Manila, in the Philippines. We all quietly listened and asked for clarification only when absolutely necessary. There was no judgment in this circle; there was only listening with our heads and hearts. Mrs. Rodriguez related her story and, in doing so, became an example of hope in collective action and a part of our lives forever.

There had been long-standing unrest and turmoil in Manila and in all of the Philippines. For years, the citizenry, who were largely poor, had stood by and watched helplessly as the president and first lady of the Philippines lived in uncontrollable royal excess. There was no hiding the amount of wealth that mysteriously grew for the first family, who seemed not to care about the people of the country. Order was enforced by authorities, and dissent was punished. There were international newspaper articles and local stories about the president and the first lady, and the Filipinos heard regularly about their lavish parties at the palaces, about celebrities, costly gifts, and an opulence that did not include them.

When she looked at her children and her friends' children, Mrs. Rodriguez realized how little hope there was for her or her country. It was the same for everyone. Throughout their history, tyrants and dictators who claimed to be leaders of the people had been exploiting the country. Finally, she said, it became unbearable. Informal leaders in neighborhoods, in concert with their local service and religious groups, began to organize.

When the uprising began, she felt compelled to do whatever she could. She vowed that the military would scare her no longer: "There was no sleep for me or anyone else. To rest meant accepting tyranny. To rest meant the end of freedom for me and my children."

We were spellbound, listening to her.

She said, "My job was organizing my neighborhood and coordinating with adjacent neighborhoods in an attempt to stop the military and their tanks from entering the city. I was to create a system of signals to coordinate communication between the different neighborhoods in Manila, so that the poor, young, and old would know where to gather on the streets."

She told us that at the signal from their organizers, they were to leave their homes and lie down in the streets in nonviolent protest. "I was terrified that even with our bodies lying in the streets, the military with their tanks and rifles would not stop, but we had no other resource as powerful as our own bodies and spirits." In the event that radio communication was cut off, they created signals with clothes and clotheslines, on the roofs of buildings, to relay where and when the tanks were coming.

On the second day, she realized the bishop and the others on the radio, who were directing the opposition to the military, had no food. She took it upon herself to remedy this. She did her best to find food, but the situation was desperate. Stores were not open. She had nothing in her cupboards. She continued searching. She looked at us and said, "Oh, then I found the colonel!"

We looked at each other, confused. She continued.

"I found the colonel!"

I could not stand it. I blurted out, "The colonel—was he on the people's side? Was he part of the military?"

"No, no! The colonel would be able to provide food for the bishop and the others!"

Seeing that we were all confused, Mrs. Rodriguez explained again that she had forgotten to plan the food for the bishop and his aides. She said, "I was so upset when I realized that we hadn't thought of everything. Here they were, working night and day and they had no food. The colonel," she continued, "the colonel was the colonel from Kentucky Fried Chicken, one of the only restaurants still open." We all burst into laughter.

She quickly regained her composure and continued her story. She got whatever food she could from the colonel and made her way to the radio station, with help from many different people along the way. She left the food for the bishop and his aides and then returned to the streets to stand at her post in unity with the others. She stood in unity with those who were hungry, who knew that justice should be theirs if they remained united together.

This uprising did not just happen. It had taken weeks of planning and the sacrifice of many for their plan to become reality.

The tanks pulled back when the people stormed the palace grounds. They rushed at the helicopter as the president and first lady made their escape. People tried to reach it as it lifted off, trying to bring it down with their bare hands. Mrs. Rodriguez said that if ever people wished they could fly, she believed it was that day.

As she finished, we were silent and watched her breathing excitedly. We were all amazed at how brave and inventive this quiet woman had been and the role she had played. She and her fellow Filipinos had banded together courageously to change their world. We had just heard a moving example of the power of unity.

After a few moments of silence, I thanked her and asked what she thought was the most important part of the role she had played. She said very quickly, "It was to fulfill a need." Finding the food for the bishop and his aides had made her so happy.

There was a pause and then she beamed with tears in her eyes, as she said she had forgotten to tell us that hours after she delivered the food, she heard her name over the radio. She heard the voice of her bishop say, "Thank you, Mrs. Rodriguez, for the colonel."

HOW CAN I TRUST IN THE GIFT OF UNITY?

Trust is a practice. It is not easy, especially for those who have been hurt deeply and routinely. And yet, many indigenous people, some of the most wronged people on the planet, continue to be stewards of people, earth, and spirit to ensure that current and future generations of human beings and other species will survive and be happy as we were meant to be. When we open our senses to what is within ourselves and support the world around us, we see the reality that unity is at work. The power of unity is sustaining us.

One of the ways to create and grow this trust in unity is to begin each day as I was taught by my Elders, by my mother, by my grandmother, and by her grandmother. Each morning, I express appreciation and gratitude for the people, the earth, nature, and spirit. I stand and, turning to the four directions, I say, "Thank you to the winds as they circle around the world touching and connecting everyone and everything. Thank you, Great Spirit, Grandmother and Grandfather, for breath. Thank you, Mother Earth, for providing us with nourishment."

With every glass of water I drink and every meal I eat, I pause and give thanks to all involved in getting these resources to my table. I thank the water, the seeds, the earth, the people who sowed and harvested and delivered and prepared the food. In this way I remind myself of the abundance that I am part of. Every day and every night, I look for opportunities to express my gratitude for the life I live and my work in unity with others.

There are so many different ways we can assist this unity and help evolution move forward. Personal acts and rituals of gratitude are wonderful, and we can also be involved in collective ceremonies and celebrations, practicing gratitude within a community. This community gratitude can happen at meals, in celebrations of life passages like birthdays, weddings, and anniversaries, and at solstices, equinoxes, plantings, and harvests.

We can celebrate and learn from the positive changes we have made. We can draw inspiration from the stories of others, like the story of the young indigenous women of Standing Rock, the story of Mrs. Rodriguez in the Philippines, and the new stories we are hearing of businesses developing the power of unity in the workplace, among their employees, and in their support of other communities. Stories not of greed but of owners sharing very prosperous businesses, giving employees a percentage of ownership, like Publix Super Markets, the Lifetouch photography company, Gore-Tex, and the New Belgium Brewing Company, making it a priority to care for one another.

As an individual, how do I begin my own transformation? Gratitude is but one of the first steps. Another is to practice empathy, a caring response to another person's emotional, physical, and spiritual state; a way of being in unity with another being. How do we practice empathy? We first imagine ourselves in the other's place, seeing through their eyes and holding them in the most positive possible light. We notice, feel into, let ourselves understand their emotions, and we care about and value them. In fact, we carry with us an intent to maximize the other's emotional well-being. This is a golden path to empathy.

Look around you; notice others who are really present to the people around them. They are bringing a healing energy to community. Watch and listen, experience their empathy, and discover how it affects you just in being present for it. From this, we can grow our own capacity to live in the empathetic state of unity with others.

THE POWER OF CONNECTION

Sometimes to understand and to acknowledge your part in a circle within the power of unity requires you to open yourself up, to really be present without judgment, and to just listen.

I will never forget designing and facilitating this major workshop experience for a multinational company. What a challenge and honor to create a process to bring together two groups of people who are often at odds with each other. Most if not all of us have had this experience in our work life: not sensing any unity between coworkers. Here is how the Gift of Unity was used in a work environment; the multinational company was DuPont and the two different culture groups were the Puerto Ricans and the largely white Americans from the state of Delaware.

The problem is that these two groups sometimes forgot that they were part of the same organization with the same goals. Due to their different ways of culturally approaching the workplace and relationships, they regularly experienced miscommunications and misunderstandings that were creating difficult issues between the teams and dragging their performance down. Our goal was to help them become more unified in order to meet their goals and objectives. It was also an opportunity to use indigenous wisdom in a workplace setting, working not only on the physical and mental levels but on the emotional and spiritual levels as well. The unity that comes from a healthy community can only occur and be sustainable by continually acknowledging that development and growth are happening at all the levels for the individual and the group. This is an indigenous principle, which the leaders agreed to and wanted to cultivate in the company.

The day of the workshop begins when the attendees enter the meeting room in an exclusive Puerto Rican resort on Dorado Beach. The room, with its tall white walls and huge windows, looks out at vibrant green palm trees and tropical flowers of every color.

Thirty business leaders, fifteen primarily white men from the corporate headquarters in Delaware and fifteen Latinos from Puerto Rico, greet each other in their own predictable way. Those from Delaware, who were called "Northerners," greet each other and the Latinos with a brisk handshake. The Latinos return the Northerners' handshakes, followed by drawing them toward them with a hug accompanied by a kiss on each cheek.

I observe one Northerner—a medium-built, six-foot-tall man—who is the first to notice that I arranged the seating into concentric circles to create an indigenous talking circle rather than using the typical classroom rows. I watch him, then scan the perimeter of the room where two long tables hold thirty lit candles, each floating in its own bowl filled with water. He also seems to notice that, just in case, we also have a fire extinguisher in each corner of the room as another safety precaution.

He shakes his head slightly and quickly sits down at the very edge of the outermost circle. Although I do not share this information early on, the water and the lit candles are present in acknowledgment of the belief that we are part of the Great Mystery, spiritual beings represented by the light in a physical body made up of sacred water.

This three-day international team-building workshop begins with the goal of creating shared work team agreements on how to be more effective in collaboration, decision-making, and exceeding their business targets in their agricultural business. The team members are committed to their business goals, and their conversations are lively, yet many of the key issues remain unaddressed at the close of day one. The participants express positive comments but also relief that they have two more days to accomplish their goals.

The six-foot-tall Northerner raises his hand and asks, "I do not want to speak impolitely, but I couldn't help notice that there are a lot of candles in water surrounding us. What are the candles for?"

Appreciating his curiosity and his willingness to ask, I smile and slowly gaze at each of the participants and respond, "This work we are doing is very important. We are attempting to understand the power of our unity and the potential for our extraordinary collaboration. To create a powerful relationship across cultures requires not just bringing your past experiences with you, and not just your dreams and visions for the future. To become the best cross-cultural colleagues and partners requires each of us to bring our higher selves. The lit candles are reminders to bring the light of our higher selves." The Northerner looks thoughtful and nods his head; the rest of the room remains silent, but I notice many Latinos are smiling from ear to ear in appreciation.

The next morning, several Latino leaders arrive early. I watch as they place small statues of saints and glasses of water with pennies next to several of the lit candles. These represent *santería*, positive energies from Christian and indigenous West African traditions.

Everyone enters the room and sits in the concentric circles. The outer circles have been designated for listening only and to hold safely the energy of the discussion within. The inner circle is reserved for those speaking. As soon as the session begins, several Northerners from Delaware who were quiet the day before quickly move into the innermost circle, talking about how it was sometimes difficult communicating with the Latinos. "We're always uncertain whether a task is really going to get done. What does *mañana* actually mean? Does it mean tomorrow, next week, next month, or what?"

Several Latinos then enter the talking circle and reply, "Before defining *mañana*, you know that we have always gotten the job done. But we have needed to periodically adjust timelines because you Northerners sometimes have unrealistic deadlines." Another adds, "Why is it that Northerners can change dates regularly and no one questions these changes? Does 'tomorrow' mean tomorrow, or will it mean a totally different day? Yet when we Spanish-speaking partners say *mañana*, it causes such distrust and confusion."

The spirited conversations go on.

Someone else says, "It is hard for me to understand why we can't be more open to each other. Even in our greeting yesterday, many of us who are friends and colleagues had not seen each other for several years, yet you stick out your hand. We Latinos shake your extended hand, but when we go to hug you, you become stiff like boards. We do not want to make you uncomfortable; we want you to know that we care. It is our custom with both women and men. We give a hug and a quick kiss on each cheek. It's not sexual. It is an acknowledgment of our connection, our unity, our relationship."

Well, this fully unleashes the conversation. It grows more animated as other serious topics are discussed; specifics about how they could work together in a better way and let go of past misunderstandings and insults to each other's dignity.

Suddenly I notice the six-foot Northerner sitting in the outer circle. His leg is nervously bouncing up and down. He looks as if he is about to jump out of his seat. I make up a story that his entire body is wanting to say: *This is all nonsense! Let's get to work!*

I smile at him, nodding my head toward the inner circle. His leg continues to bounce up and down in his chair. Before I can ask him if he wishes to join the inner talking circle, he blurts out, "I can't stand it anymore!"

The lively conversation stops. All eyes are on him.

"I'm sorry! I just cannot stand it anymore!" Pointing to one of the side tables, he shouts, "That candle is about to go out!"

There is a second of silence and perhaps surprise, and then everyone laughs in relief.

I ask the man to tell us what is happening inside of him.

"If that lit candle and those other objects that have appeared around the room are going to help us to work better together and respect each other, then keep the darn candles lit!"

With a smile, I take a match and relight the candle.

There have been times in workshops when I have wanted to give a big hug, in front of everyone, to a participant for leading the transformation. This is one of those times.

Most of the Northerners, unlike the Latinos, did not completely understand those candles, let alone the statues and pennies. However, that one Northerner actually did understand that there is also a power or energy greater than what we can always sense, and when the candle was about to go out, he bravely owned that he could not stand it anymore. He acknowledged that we are in a sacred space.

Being silent was not his choice. He made it safe for everyone to not just tolerate but to value cultural differences and begin to openly talk about them. If the candles—spirit—are going to help us be more successful by understanding the power of our unity—the light and connection—then let us keep them lit for the benefit of all, both Latinos from Puerto Rico and Northerners from Delaware.

The next day we have the closing ceremony, in which each person writes down the completion of two sentences and each takes a turn sharing in the speaking circle. The first sentence completion is: "A stereotype or bias that I brought with me to this meeting was . . ." and they then describe it. Followed with: "I tear this up and throw it away, carrying it no longer." They throw the paper with this statement into a bowl, understanding that all of these statements will be burned later in an outdoor fire.

Next, they complete the second sentence: "One thing I learned about myself, my culture, or your culture that I am taking with me is . . ." Each person will keep this second commitment.

After this part of the ceremony is complete, the Latinos stand together. One woman steps forward and says: "We have something to tell you Northerners. We thought you were taller than us, but we were mistaken. What we know now is that you are not. We realize that we have been kneeling down. Now we are standing up alongside of you to work together in unity, connected as true partners."

The six-foot Northerner is the first one to give a hug and a peck on the cheek of each of the Latino coworkers. As all the candles continue to burn, the room is filled with tears of joy, laughter, and hugs—the power of unity.

In this story, people from different cultures were able to understand their interconnection and come to a mutually beneficial unity through listening as well as speaking in the circle. The bond between the people from different cultural backgrounds grew strong with this new awareness and acceptance of their connections, and with this renewed sense of empowerment they exceeded their business goals and objectives for years to come.

THE UNITY OF A MISSION

Another example that illustrates the power of connecting and recognizing how each individual, each position, each task, whether small or big, contributes to the whole and the larger mission is my experience in Thailand, where I am facilitating an all-team meeting with EarthRights International, a nongovernmental, nonprofit organization that combines the power of law and the power of people in defense of human rights and the environment, which they define as "earth rights."

They are creating a five-year plan, and they are doing it not by looking at problems but rather by looking at what has worked well. They are asking and considering what they have already learned to do, what can be created, and what is their shared vision and dream. They recognize that a sign of their success comes from supporting the power of people with the power of law in their country and elsewhere, and using the law to work with native communities to maintain their cultures and the health of the lands they are part of. They have also stated that they want to win the Nobel Peace Prize.

Some employees were doubtful, thinking: *Well, they just want us to work harder*. But nonetheless, this small group of employees in a small organization began sharing their stories, and they continued to all three days of the session. At the end of the first day, a young man, about twenty-one, who had been very quiet raises his hand. The group turns to listen to him.

He says, "I don't know if you've noticed, I'm the only one who has not spoken today, but I'd like to speak now." We all smile and nod.

He says, "I've been driving a taxi since I was fourteen. I picked people up and dropped them off and picked people up and dropped them off. That's basically what I did. In this organization, you hired me to go pick up people at the border of Burma, bring them here, and take them back, no questions.

"I pick up people, drop them off, and pick them up, just like I did before. What I've come to understand here is that I'm far more than just this one lonely taxi driver. I'm bringing people from across the border here to learn how to unite people, and then returning them to the border to spread this collective work. I'm an important part of a freedom movement. A movement that makes this place a place that works for all of us."

He saw the power of connection, what the power of unity can achieve. He was conscious that his actions were part of fulfilling a larger, meaningful purpose, which uplifted the entire team's purpose. They each now understood that it was not about doing more work or singling out individual work; it was about uniting and working together in service to a greater mission: that of helping indigenous people and their lands around the world. Indeed, each one hugged him during the break, saying, "We are glad to be together in this freedom movement." EarthRights has not yet won the Nobel Peace Prize, but several years after implementing their five-year strategic plan, the founder, Ka Hsaw Wa, was awarded the Ramon Magsaysay Award, which is a counterpart of the Nobel Peace Prize for Asia.

In these stories, we can see there is joy in discovering our unity with others, our inextricable connection to who they are, what they do, and our journey together in this life. A wonderful wholeness can emerge, for as we embrace our unity with other beings, we also strengthen our unity with the land and with spirit. Aware of all our relations, we deepen our connection to the one.

Allow me to be able to release negative energies from my body and my heart, as the volcanoes cleanse the waters to be drinkable.

Set me free, Sacred K'at, from restrictions of my mind and heart. Then I will be free to share my inner peace and to shelter others in the Web of Love that you represent, Sacred K'at.

Make me an instrument of peace to open paths of reconciliation and tolerance in my community, in my country, and this Sacred Planet that is our home.

—NANA MARÍA CHIQUI RAMIREZ, AYQ'IJ,
MAYAN TIMEKEEPER, GUATEMALA

THE MEDICINE OF UNITY

As part of my daily ritual, I go into nature, which may mean just standing next to a flower or a tree on a busy city block or, at home, going out into the foothills of the Rocky Mountains where the pine forests and lichen-covered stones are plentiful. Here is a oneness-with-nature meditation:

Please go stand or sit in nature. Allow yourself to be drawn to something of nature—a tree, for example. Then take three cleansing breaths. With each breath, allow your mind to become present to the tree right now, free of any worries or thoughts; you might imagine a whiteboard in your mind and wiping off those worries or thoughts.

When you feel present, ask the spirit of the tree to allow you to connect with its essence. Focus on the tree and use each of your five senses one at a time, almost in slow motion.

First, look at the tree, really seeing it, and take its visual presence into every cell of your body. Pause.

Then touch the tree and register what it feels like, bringing the feeling of its essence into every cell of your body. Pause.

With the softest part of your ear, listen to the sound of the tree and take that sound, its tone, into every cell of your body. Pause.

Now smell the scent, the perfume of the tree, and take that smell into every cell of your body. Pause.

Then imagine the taste of the tree and take the essence of the taste into every cell of your body. Pause.

Be aware and open to the senses of connection and peace.

It is so pure that you may feel, with time, as if you could be one with the tree and it is one with you.

With practice, you will sense the peace-filled quickening effect on your spirit, emotions, mind, and physical state, for each time you practice this meditation, you will be reminded that we are always in sacred space, connected to all life. Enjoy consciously, discovering nature's life-giving connection to you.

5

The Third Sacred Gift:
The Power of Healing

*Naku, which means "forest" in the Sápara language, is an
urgent call to the world to heal the spirit world and, by
virtue of this, to heal us all. It is a call to all our human
sisters and brothers to re-immerse ourselves in this great
spirit ecology; to allow us once again to be nourished by it
as we play our role in sustaining and caring for it.*

**—MANARI USHIGUA, EMISSARY AND GUARDIAN
OF THE SÁPARA NATION OF ECUADOR**

I AM GRATEFUL TO my indigenous Elders who taught
me since I was a child to "listen with the softest part of your
ear." Through their example, I know that listening is the most
important thing you can do for someone. It is a responsibility
and an act of care and love.

How do you listen with the softest part of your ear? The
answer takes me back to one memorable, marathon-length

women's talking circle where my Elder showed me how to listen.

I lean forward in my hard-backed chair, trying to find a comfortable position with my round, eight-months-pregnant belly. Even though sitting for hours may be difficult, I know that it is important for me to be here. Thirty-five women from twenty-eight tribes—ages seventeen to seventy years of age, black- to light-haired, a range of brown to blue eyes—settle into our chairs, creating a circle.

The silver-haired Dr. Henrietta Mann, Southern Cheyenne and ceremonial leader, rises from her chair and speaks: "Each of you is brilliant and carry the medicine of our people. We are healing medicine to each other. We do not need to stay locked into those areas where we feel anger, danger, hurt. When we forgive, then we can heal. This sacred circle is, for us, a healing place. Here only one person speaks at a time. We get to listen, without judgment, no commenting on what another says. If your mind starts to wander, then just open your heart wider and your ability to listen some more will happen. Our listening allows the speaker to give voice to, make sense of, and even let go of her story."

With burning sage in one hand and her eagle feather in the other, Henrietta stands in front of each one of us. I can taste, feel, smell, and see the cleansing sage wafting over each of the women and me. I see the smoke mingle together with our breathing, becoming one in the room. Henrietta returns to her chair, and now, for hours, we sit mostly in silence to give the gift of listening as each woman takes her turn to speak.

To an untrained observer it may appear as thirty-five disjointed stories. To those of us who are practiced in this community process, we know that somehow, by listening, bearing witness to another, we will all leave transformed, speakers and listeners. Sitting for hours in a circle, we begin to hear not only the words but also the silence, what I call the music between the words.

"My brother is here in the other room with the men's circle. I have been so angry at him," a teenager says with tears running down her face. "He was with his friends last spring; they were drinking and doing drugs. That night, they climbed the fence to go for a swim in the closed community swimming pool. My brother threw off his clothes and dove into the pool without realizing it had no water and split his head open like a watermelon. He would be the first to say that it is a miracle that he survived the surgeries and months of mending his broken bones.

"Receiving the love from each of you as we silently listen to each other, I feel the anger floating away with the sage. I am left here with a sense of forgiveness for myself for not being there to stop my brother's actions, and forgiveness for my brother and the pain he brought to my family and me. He has been clean for sixteen months." The circle closes. Henrietta smiles.

I can say, even being eight months pregnant, that I have been so transfixed during the last five hours listening to each of the women, I have almost forgotten to shift my position on my chair while my son moves inside my belly. The circle ends, we hug each other, then we leave the room to rejoin the men.

Listening is an essential, necessary practice for creating and sustaining relationships with others and yourself. We must listen, listen, and listen some more. As in the case of my son Alex's transformation, listening can even help heal a broken heart.

Alex was twenty years old at the time and he had just returned from a long-anticipated summer, studying music in England and visiting Italy, and then joining his girlfriend for several weeks in Asia, where she was doing a summer college internship.

Alex described his summer as "fantastic." He had saved for this dream trip for some time and it was a huge success. I was a happy parent, seeing my son, all six foot two of him, walking around as if his feet were not even touching the ground.

One day, soon after he returned, the front door opened and from upstairs I heard moaning and crying. I ran to see what had happened. It was Alex. I quickly looked for blood and, seeing none, asked, "What happened?" He said through his tears, "It hurts so bad. I can't believe it hurts so bad!"

My usual response would be to drill Alex with questions, frantic to know the cause and all the details. Instead, I remembered the Elder's advice and what I had learned. This was not the time to ask questions in order to satisfy my need for information or to focus on problem solving; it was the time to be present, grounded, and focused for my son. I kept quiet and felt my care gently reach out to him.

At last he said, "I don't know what happened! My girlfriend says she doesn't love me anymore, and she just broke up with me! I thought she was happy. I was so happy."

Sitting next to him, I said, "I am here. I am listening." My heart was aching, too. I understood that I could not fix this for my son. I reminded myself that this was about his journey as a young adult and that I could not solve his problem. What I could do was listen. Listen, listen some more, and allow him the space to figure out what to do, how to heal his own broken heart with a supportive family member present, and move forward when he was ready.

As young children, my two sons used to bring their blankets and pillows and sleep on the carpeted floor in their father's and my bedroom or just outside the door when one or both were upset. No questions were ever asked; they simply knew that we were there for them.

Alex ached so much that he began to sleep on the floor outside our room, not for days, but for weeks.

In late October, two months after the breakup, Alex announced, "I've got an appointment with the counselor at school. I've been reluctant to go to the counselor, because my friend said that the counselor usually listens and then prescribes antidepressants. I don't want pills."

I hugged him and simply said, "I'll be here," trusting in his innate good sense and ability to find his way forward.

Although he only saw the counselor for one visit, by Thanksgiving Alex was no longer sleeping on the floor by our bedroom door. He returned to his apartment near the university.

In December, Alex and I were riding in the car, and he turned to me and said, "Mom, I saw my old girlfriend." My hands tightened on the steering wheel, and I almost blurted out: *What!* Instead, I took a deep breath and said, "I'm listening."

He said, "I asked her if she would be willing to share more about what went wrong between us—not to get back together, just so that I understood." I kept looking at the road and held my tongue.

She told him, "My parents and I had a meeting and we decided that I could do better than you." I took a deep breath and continued listening.

He continued, "So I said to her, if it was about money, you know that I'll be a great businessman, but she shook her head to say 'No.'" Then Alex said with tears, "Mom, I had this feeling rise up from my gut and I said to her, 'Is it because I'm Mexican and Indian?' And this time she nodded her head 'Yes' and walked away from me."

I felt the urge to become a mama bear protecting her cub, to react to this cruel attempt to diminish my son. Instead, I continued to listen in silence, totally present for him.

About a month later, we were driving somewhere, and he turned and said, "Mom, I have something to tell you." I quickly felt scared and tightened my grip on the steering wheel.

With a big smile, he blurted out, "I love you so much! You and Dad were there for me, listening and hugging me, trusting me over these past months. You let me figure out who I am, what I want. I know now that I can deal with tough things as they come up in my life."

With a big sigh of relief, I settled into confidence that Alex has the inner strength and the wisdom to work through the challenges he faces in his life, be it racial bigotry or something else. I loosened my grip and said, "I'm listening, and I always will."

I now have a clearer understanding of how to practice the instructions from my Elders, "You must listen with the softest part of your ear to be truly present." Listening with the softest part of your ear is to listen with empathy and compassion, bringing your whole self to be present for the other. Listening is an absolutely core element that supports your use of the third sacred gift: the power of healing.

ESSENTIAL HEALING ELEMENTS

"Healing" is a very soft word that we can use to describe many things. A song can be healing, a person's touch can be healing, and a meal prepared with love can be healing.

Indigenous wisdom of healing is very different from going to the doctor to get a prescription for a condition or a health problem. Indigenous Elders always tailor their healing practices to the immediate situation. At times, they reach out to the person in need with a compassionate touch and use soft, caring words. At other times, they will fearlessly use challenging questions that cut right to the heart of the situation. And still other times they may draw on the elements of nature to bring about healing energy.

The four basic elements or practices to use in each healing situation are:

1. Listening
2. Supportive Relationships
3. Unconditional Love
4. Committing to Creative, Positive Action

These key elements ensure healing will occur. When combined, they are a most powerful gift.

LISTENING

The story of my son Alex reveals the power of listening on different levels. It was an occasion for me to practice listening as a parent with trust in him, and it was also an experience for my son to practice listening to his own heart in order to become present to what was out of balance and find his center again.

Rather than complain or blame his ex-girlfriend, Alex gave himself the time to ask himself questions and then took the time to really listen to the answers. Over the weeks and months following the breakup, he continually got in touch with what was happening in his body. The body is always giving messages to us to restore health and wholeness; it's telling us that we have to take the time to pause and listen.

Alex spoke about how he was making sense of what had happened with the breakup, and he was looking at the underlying stories that he was telling about himself and others involved. He knew that he was making up stories where he had no factual information. It was helpful to ask his ex-girlfriend, when he had the opportunity, what she perceived had happened to cause failure in their sustaining a healthy relationship.

When Alex was hurt, he turned to others for their trust and love to provide him the space and grace by listening, listening, and listening some more to him as he healed and transformed into an even stronger human being, trusting his ability to be whole. Whenever we ask ourselves, *What are the stories I am telling myself? What are the unexamined assumptions underlying those stories I create about myself and others?*, we open up the possibility to know ourselves better by getting in touch with and listening to our bodies and hearts.

To listen with the softest part of your ear is to hold an intention to listen with empathy and compassion, a practice that asks you to be mindful and heart centered so you can listen unconditionally and without judgment. When you're listening to the heart of another, here are a few steps to help you cultivate listening from the softest part of your ear:

- First, take a pause and breathe into your body, allowing the oxygen to reach from the top of your head down to the tips of your toes, be still and quiet for several seconds, and then exhale out from your heart. This repeated breathing, opening up, and then emptying oneself provides the cradle from which you can listen.

- Second, quiet your mind. For some of us, it may be like using an eraser on a whiteboard where our thoughts are written. For others, it may be releasing our thoughts, letting them float away like clouds. The key is that you focus completely on the other person's need and words and let your inner conversation dissipate. For some, choosing to immerse themselves in the experience of the other right in front of them helps to quiet the mind.

- Third, stay silent. Let go of your need to say or do anything other than being present for this person, trusting that the other person's own sacred wisdom will lead the way.

- Fourth, repeat steps one, two, and three as needed.

To listen with the softest part of our ears to our own heart, use the same four steps above, cherishing yourself as you would the other.

Listening has different qualities and tones. In observing a cat you can see where its focus is. The cat can have a sharp-focused attention in listening as it uses all its senses targeted at a toy or a mouse. Or the cat can have a wide-focused attention in listening as it relaxes on the back of the couch, taking in all of its environment.

As humans, we often listen with focused attention targeted on answers, conclusions, or our response to what another person is saying. Listening with the softest part of our ear is listening with a wide-angle attention, taking in everything the person is conveying and being present in that moment. Keep in mind that listening is not all hard; it is joyful, too.

With time emptying your mind and opening your heart to people, animals, and nature, you, too, are nourished. By listening, you acknowledge the other's and your own sacredness, which relieves suffering. It is never too early or too late to practice listening with the softest part of your ear.

One of my earliest memories of listening dates back to when I was four years old. It is the darkest time of the night, and my family is sleeping. I hear the breath of my sister, Paula, who sleeps on the cot next to me. Sounds drift from the living room, where my two brothers and parents are asleep on the sofa bed. A quiet serenade of breaths interspersed with the snores of my father, resting his body after another long day of shoveling coal into the furnaces at Armco Steel.

My little body is awake, and I am in my pajamas, bleached white and smelling fresh. It is the middle of the night, and I can hear the sky outside, which has called to me to listen. Tiptoeing on my little round feet, I grasp the peeling paint on the window-sill. I balance there, ever so still, so as not to wake Paula. I am joyful in my body as I listen to the night sky.

I can hear the starlight's twinkling messages, as if in a call-and-response between starry sisters and brothers. Their sing-song conversation has varied tempos: slow and fast, short and long. The long pauses in between some of their messages give me the sense that they are listening to one another. In response I listen deeply, motionless and quiet.

Effortlessly, I follow their conversation, their laughter, and the dance they perform. There is no need to speak; there are no restrictions of vocabulary and my ears tingle with the brilliant sounds of a sky that is alive and glorious. I am thrilled by this awareness of the universe, of a community with others in the dark and of life unfolding. I feel the depth of the sky and its messages. I am witness to the truths that are being shared tonight. I am listening, healing, listening, healing, listening. . . .

This is a perfect example of what our elders tell us: that if we quiet ourselves and really listen to the natural world around us, we will find that we are part of an enormous, beautiful community. A place to be reminded of our wholeness and heal in that nurturing embrace.

SUPPORTIVE RELATIONSHIPS

From the foundation of listening comes our capacity to build honest relationships. These supportive bonds give us the strength to heal what we need to heal in ourselves and to accept support from other beings—people, nature, and spirit.

For healing to occur, it needs the presence, acknowledgment, and support of another person. It doesn't have to be an expert or therapist who has all the answers to solve your problem; real transformation in healing happens because of what the person themself is doing. When another person listens to you and supports you in your healing, they act as a witness with an open heart to mirror the changes you are going through. This witness and mirror can be another human being or a being from nature or a presence in spirit, as we will see below.

ALAN'S JOURNEY: HEALING THROUGH THE HEART AND BODY

We can see a brilliantly effective demonstration of this wisdom, this understanding, in the healing process known as RIM (Regenerating Images in Memory), created by Dr. Deb Sandella. Through RIM's focus on a person's innate wholeness, rather than human brokenness, and by trusting in that person's natural inner wisdom, we can help them awaken to their own healing. We can be the witness and neutral guide to their self-directed healing journey.

Alan is a bright young man in his mid-twenties who I hire to help me create some videos. During the filming, I am aware of his serious, subdued nature. In addition to his fee, I offer to gift him a RIM session.

We are sitting in my home office with lots of warm sunlight filling the room. Alan proceeds to tell me that his company isn't growing because, as he explains, "I have the hardest time trusting others to help me. I want to grow the number of film projects, but my turnaround time is so slow. I am uncomfortable delegating."

I tell Alan a few things about the RIM process: "I will be your supportive, neutral guide, following you as you listen to your body, images, feelings, and messages from your actual memories or imagined ones. We will trust and follow whatever comes up. You will remain conscious and aware of what is going on the entire time. Therefore, Alan, you can't do anything wrong."

"I'm a little nervous. I've never done this before, but I am open to what shows up," Alan replies. We begin.

"Alan, close your eyes and notice your breath, notice your body releasing tension from a deeper and deeper place with each exhale. Scan your body and tell me when you sense something show up or draw your attention; it may show up as tension, discomfort, darkness, or light—whatever."

With his eyes closed, he begins to breathe deeply, and his stomach grabs his attention. He feels like vomiting and begins to cry.

I say, "Alan, use your imagination and bring in a resource

to be here with you—someone or something that provides you safety and wisdom."

"My childhood golden retriever, Max, is beside me."

"How does that feel?"

"Really good. I trust Max the most." With Max's spirit by his side as his virtual resource, I ask Alan for them to go together into the nauseous space in his stomach and tell me what he senses.

"It's me, I'm six years old, I'm beside a lake fishing with my dad, and Max is beside me.

"I am going deeper into the nauseous feeling in my gut. I sense that my not trusting lives here," he continues. "Oh no, I can't hold on to the fishing pole. I drop it into the lake. My dad is scrambling to recover it and he can't. I'm crying." Alan has tears streaming down his cheeks as he continues to describe his dad yelling at him for losing the expensive rod. His dad angrily says, "I should know better. If I want something done right, I have to do it myself. I can't trust anyone. Alan, you have to do things right. You're old enough now."

Alan is crying and feeling sad that his dad is so furious with him. Finding this sadness in his little body, he embraces it and through tears he apologizes: "Dad, I'm so sorry, I didn't mean to lose the pole. It just slipped through my hands. I don't even know how." Feeling through the sadness, Alan eventually remembers that his dad did apologize when they returned home. I sit silently observing and listening.

Alan says that the six-year-old wishes to be with his dad, and then he says, "Dad, I forgive you. I know you didn't mean to hurt me. You were worried about the money. I understand."

Alan then looks at Max and feels good remembering his dog's unconditional love. I prompt Alan with the question "What wants to happen next?" Alan sees himself as a couple years younger than his current age of twenty-eight. Sensing Max still by his side, he feels different, his stomach doesn't hurt, and there's something bringing his attention to his belly. I say, "Alan, go into that sensation. What do you find?"

With Max, Alan feels inside his belly and discovers an open space that's "sensory, not visual." In this space, he feels safe creating anything he wants. He and Max romp and play freely until Alan senses Max say: "I love you, Alan. You trusted me, and you still do. I went to school with you and then was free to do whatever I wanted. I was always there for you." Alan tearfully receives the dog's love like a ribbon of light that fills his body with sensations of comfort and trust.

I ask, "Is there anything else that needs to happen?"

Alan asks, "Can I keep Max?"

"Yes, of course!" I reply.

Reassured that Max will always be there to fill him with love and trust, the filmmaker eventually opens his eyes.

After the RIM session, Alan says, "I'm a bit weirded out and surprised how deeply emotional this was for me. Everything was so real, vivid." He smiles then and adds, "You did tell me that we would trust and follow whatever I had come up in me. It didn't address my issue of delegating, so I can get more projects, but I am a perfect ten on feeling loved."

A month later, I received a call from the colleague who had

connected Alan and me: "I don't know what you did to Alan, but he's totally different. He's gotten two big projects since the session and has hired lots of new people to help him. Oh, and he's fallen in love. He trusts his people so much that now he's off enjoying free time with his new girlfriend. When he was my student, he never played because he was overly responsible."

The intensity of six-year-old Alan's sadness caused his dad's comments to anchor unconsciously in Alan's young brain. Because the RIM method of listening and guiding is a non-intellectual process that produces beneficial results without logical thinking, Alan's mind initially didn't see the connection between his dad's saying "I can't trust anyone" and his own discomfort in delegating.

By connecting to his body, he allowed his imagination to recall and re-create this critical moment, and by working through the experience with healing statements, this process precipitated an organic change that effectively addressed his stated problem. Alan's experience demonstrates how the presence of another can provide witness to someone who is identifying self-limiting thoughts and feelings. By erasing old, deep-seated thoughts, he was able to make behavioral changes even without intellectually understanding what was happening.

Although there is training specific to the RIM process, you don't have to be trained in order to be receptive to another with a similar kind of supportive energy and intent. Grounded in a belief in the other's fundamental wholeness and innate healing wisdom, you can sit with someone, without an agenda, holding supportive space as they explore old stories, blocked emotions, and limiting beliefs. Just by being there for someone, as a witness and mirror, you frame a safe container for another to do their work. This is the healing that comes through your supportive relationship.

RELATIONSHIP: DRAWING ON THE HEALING POWER OF NATURE

As children, when my siblings and I got wound up and started picking on each other, my mom would tell us to go outside. She sent us out of the house not just to get rid of us but because she knew that once we stepped on the earth or sat next to a tree or started moving, a natural process of healing would take place. This connection to earth is essential. So often I've witnessed myself and other adults benefit from a pause in the business at hand to retreat to the outdoors for reflection and rejuvenation.

In the Amazon rain forest, the indigenous peoples draw directly on nature for healing. They have cures for broken bones, cuts, wounds, and fevers that come from various plants, water, and minerals. The healing process reflects the indigenous belief that life is interconnected and everything needed is available within and around us, which is evidenced by the healing that occurs from the use of plants and their energies and properties.

The synergy of how the healing happens is generally not linear; it is circular, like a medicine wheel. I do not know if science will ever understand all of it, or that it is meant to. We *can* understand this gift of healing as both an internal process and an external process—healing that is most potent when it draws from our connection and engagement with all the different elements from the natural, human, and spiritual worlds.

Some Elders have particular gifts of drawing on nature for healing. I think often of Grandma Ruth, a healer I have known who used the spirit of fire to cure illnesses and heal injuries on the physical level. Yet, like every indigenous healer I've ever met, when she worked with a person, she was not only healing on a physical level but also cleansing the person's emotional, mental, and spiritual energies. When we bring nature into our self-recovery, we should remember to open our whole selves to healing—body, mind, and spirit.

How do we bring nature into our self-recovery? If you will take the time to be still and listen, your spirit has the answer. Your spirit may look to a tree for strength, you may let your spirit soar high into the sky with a bird, you may lie in the grass and let your consciousness travel the canyons between the clouds, you may gaze upon the stars and ask them to hold your troubles, you may allow yourself to be repainted by a sunset. Whenever you ask for nature's help and allow yourself to be guided by nature, your spirit will answer and find the way.

RELATIONSHIP: THE HEALING POWER OF COMMUNITY

Another of the many facets of healing in relationships is being a part of a community where a group of people is sharing in a ritual or activity. For me, at powwows and spiritual cleansing and healing ceremonies and listening to the drums work on the deeper parts of my psyche, something happens to create a reverberation inside me, and the group's energy finds the hidden, unconscious places I have stored pain, healing them in ways that seem impossible through conventional therapy alone.

Unfortunately, healing through ceremony in community is a foreign concept for most of today's culture. Most of our modern-day, non-indigenous group ceremonies are centered around ball games, vacations, holidays, feasts, and celebrations with minimal intention or sacredness. We need intention; it is the intentional part of our ceremonies that harnesses energy and creates the possibility for healing and happiness. The healing power comes from a shared sense of the sacred.

What I have witnessed time and time again is that healing almost always occurs in the company of others who are keenly focused on a sacred intention of care and support where healing is wanted. The members of this community call on their connection to each other and all their relations. They acknowledge spirit in their own cultural tradition; they may call on the elements of water, earth, air, fire, or light. They employ ritual and practice that speaks to them, such as a talking circle, dance, or meditation. The teachings of my Elders always show up in the most basic values of people's life-giving relationships to each other. When people are relating to each other through goodwill, honesty, and caring, then the healing energy of relationship naturally takes over and positive things happen.

Watching groups of people who choose to be kind and caring to each other confirms the power of this gift of healing. The healing source is within you and around us; you only need to recognize and tap into this abundant source. By creating positive experiences in community, you can embody the inseparable connection to people, earth, and spirit.

HEALING IS IN UNCONDITIONAL LOVE

Unconditional love is our greatest treasure. We must find a seed of it inside ourselves that we protect. We can then support it to grow stronger through the process of healing without judgment, blame, shame, or separateness. It is a fundamental mind-set, the deep meaning of all my relations—embodied in the indigenous belief and worldview that we are here in the light of creation and all beings have a right to be loved.

Each of us is worthy of unconditional love by virtue of being alive. Often, we act as if this unconditional love never or rarely exists, yet my experience is that unconditional love is ever present through cultivating our connection to all our relations. The healing power of unconditional love can be a simple loving hug from a grandparent, or sometimes spirit mysteriously provides an experience of unconditional love that creates deep healing of old wounds and traumas that opens a person to rebirth at all levels.

THE FOREVER-LIGHT

My sleep has always been precious to me. I can dependably retreat to sleep: it is a place of safety and nourishment and, most of all, one where vivid dreams can fully awaken my spirit and inform my conscious mind. My dreams are usually in full color and high definition.

As a result of this, I have always been eager to go to sleep and get my eight to nine hours per night. Yet, when I was nineteen, for several months I found myself awakened every night with a nightmare. I would go to sleep and, shortly afterward, I would awaken in tears, my heart pounding.

I would sit bolt upright, possessed with the images of an olive-skinned, curly dark-haired doll tumbling from the sky. I felt totally helpless and breathless, holding my chest for fear that I would not be able to breathe again.

Every night for months, the dream interrupted my sleep, over and over and over again. A dark shadow had invaded my most personal and private space. Sleep was a necessity, so each night I would return to sleep fearful of the images that awaited me. My roommate and college friends attempted to comfort me. They offered their best interpretations of this nightmarish dream, but no Freudian or New Age interpretation could lessen my anxiety.

When I was a child, my mom taught me to always ask the Elders and spirit guides—those who had already passed—and earthly beings—those who are living—for an explanation of my dreams. In the past, these explanations always seemed to come in clear whispers, colors, sensations, and images, the very personal internal language that blossomed in me over years of opening to my dreams. Like the indigenous dream cultures, such as the Achuar, I had come to intuitively recognize that my dreams and my waking life are intimately interwoven, not separate.

This time, no clear message, no dawning insight, came from my dream guides, but the images were unmistakable. Night after night, a series of dark, detailed snapshots of the falling doll filled my mind and upset my heart. I saw a medium-size house with white clapboard siding and a gray wooden porch. The porch was raised and had wooden steps leading up to it. Crumbled remains of a cement walkway ran beneath the length of the porch and led to these stairs. Subsequent images showed the walkway that crossed the small front yard, mostly dirt with patches of grass. The house seemed harmless enough—a place where an ordinary Midwestern family would live.

Each night, the image of the house appeared with its windows shiny clean and sunlight bouncing off of them. I could see no sign of the family who lived there. Surely the doll belonged to someone in this home, and I was aware how desperately I wanted to tell someone to rescue the doll.

Each night, the dark-haired doll tumbled out of the sky. This continued for weeks, until one night my response to the dream changed. The change was as abrupt as flipping on a light switch.

On this night, instead of being possessed by fear and anxiety, I saw a miraculous light. It appeared to emanate from within and outside every part of the doll's body. The light reflected on every facet of the house, the cement walkway, the yard, the tufts of grass—everything, even the sky. This changed everything. Now, every night, I wanted to remain asleep so that I could see and feel this brilliant white light that surrounded everything, was a part of everything, and seemed to go on forever.

It was different from sunlight. I called it "forever-light."

The stream of still images became a motion picture and I was there, too. Each time, the fall ended with the curly-haired doll hitting the hard cement. I sensed the painful impact, which passed quickly, giving way to this dazzling forever-light permeating everything. The light emanated from within and all around me.

In this timeless moment, I felt a sense of peace about the falling doll. The light was now everywhere and everything. In the company of the falling doll, I was allowed to enter this peaceful place. I was at peace.

Then, suddenly, the light was gone and a terrified baby's scream filled the dream. I woke up in bed, shaken and yet yearning to return to the powerful light.

Since childhood, I had always talked to my mom and shared with her what I experienced in my dreams, and she would share hers, too. I was so excited about this amazing nightmare that had become this wonderful dream, I knew I had to call her right away. I called her—*Oh, please pick up the phone!*—but Mom did not answer; she was not home.

Almost reluctantly, I called my sister, Paula, who always seemed to be too busy to talk. This time, however, she was free, and when I told her about the dream, she began to cry. Paula said through her tears, "I'm so sorry. I was little. I was supposed to be watching you. You were eleven months old, and I was playing and didn't know that you rolled off the porch."

"What?" I responded. "The doll, the baby, was me?"

"Yes," said Paula. Still crying, she mumbled a mix of apology and complaint about the unfairness of being responsible for me and my other siblings because she was the oldest girl. "It's hard being the oldest. I thought you had died. You didn't cry; you were lying there on the cement, not moving. I knew that I was in big trouble. I didn't mean for this to happen to you."

I wanted her to stop so I could tell her about the light. Finally, she blew her nose, giving me a chance to tell her about the rest of the dream: "Paula, there was the most brilliant light. It's a loving light, full of the amazing energy that we all are, and we don't have to wait, we can know it. I *know* it!" I'm not sure that Paula fully believed me, but I'm so glad that she answered my call.

This was not just a dream. It was a stored experience of a real event. It was telling me what I needed to remember from when I was just eleven months old. In the dream, the fall seemed like a death, but it was actually a rebirth, a process of healing and growth.

The dream didn't mean that I wouldn't die at some point, but it did give me an unforgettable experience of a deep, all-penetrating, love-filled light that made me profoundly aware that I am here for a purpose.

From that core experience, in my heart I believe that each of us is here for a purpose in this journey of wholeness, healing, and rebirth. I feel that none of us is alone; no one's life is insignificant. The profound experience of the forever-light created a rebirth and gave me another chance to live my life. Since that time, I feel closer to everything and everyone, and this abundance that we are a part of, that I experience, is proof for me that we exist as an amazing interconnection of energy, light, peace, joy, and love.

With certainty, I know that this brilliant, loving light was the Great Spirit, as my indigenous Elders have described, or God, as my Catholic teachers would say. If this dream showed me what death or rebirth really means—to cross from earthly life to the other side—I imagine that I will not fear my actual death.

I would have been more attentive, even transfixed, by religious studies had the nuns been able to share with me this perspective on life. This forever-light is the connection to all life, the connection to all my relations, the connection to those who came before, those who are present, and those still to come.

We are all one, we are all light, we are all energy.

Each of us can draw healing from our dreams. For some, a deep practice of meditation achieves the awareness of being part of the healing light. For others, ceremonial and sacred dance is the key. You might try the practice I use for preparing myself to draw wisdom from my dreams: Before I go to sleep, I quiet myself and feel the connection to all my relations, the world around and within me. I imagine the presence of my spirit guides, anyone or anything that brings me safety and wisdom, and ask them to bring knowledge and understanding that will be of service to others and me and to help me remember what I am to know. Upon awakening, I surround myself with my guides, asking them to whisper my learnings back to me, and then I thank them. Sometimes I ask my guides to remain with me during the day to help me faithfully act on the dream wisdom.

HEALING IS IN COMMITTING TO CREATIVE, POSITIVE ACTION

Committing to creative, positive action is a person's decision to tell their story in a way that focuses on choices they can make: how they can apply unconditional love to themselves by always bringing themselves back to self-acceptance, happiness, and joy. If you can do the hard work of healing, then ultimately that process brings you experiences of peace and joy—if not during the journey, then definitely at the end, when it returns us to our natural state of wholeness.

There is a huge, deep well of joy in my life and a large well of pain. I have needed to know both of them intimately. Do you also have a well of joy? And a well of pain?

There were times in my life when I believed and acted as if my well of pain was so much larger than my well of joy. It felt as if my joy was almost nonexistent. This is what trauma can do to us. It talks the loudest and screams for attention.

Yet indigenous Elders, their ceremonies, teachings, and practices, affirm that all life is sacred and spiritually connected. When we acknowledge this connection and commit to positive actions, we can discover that our well of joy is truly infinite in size. One example of positive action grounded in spiritual connection is the story of how I was able to finally write my doctoral dissertation.

SOARING LIKE AN EAGLE

I painted everything in my house, including the kitchen cabinets, taking four months to do so, in order to avoid writing my dissertation. In excusing my procrastination, I told myself that I had already accomplished so much, done so many good things in my life, and would continue to do so. I had overcome many real barriers, including economic poverty, childhood sexual abuse, the death of a parent, race and gender discrimination. I thought to myself, *Do I really need to have a doctoral degree? Do I really have what it takes to finish this?*

When I ran out of house painting to do, I got angry. Crying and shouting at God, Grandmother and Grandfather, I said, "Why are you making me do this doctorate? I'm tired. I'll continue to do good in the world even if I don't get this degree. I still promise to care about social change. I'm not going to abandon my work of advocating for those who do not have access, advocating for justice, for the rights of people and nature. Women, people of all races, will still get my attention. With others, I'll create environments where life can thrive, where each of us can contribute our gifts and receive gifts."

As I stood on my back deck overlooking the snowcapped peaks of the Continental Divide, I continued my tirade. "Okay, God, Grandmother and Grandfather, if you want me to write this dissertation, then you must give me a sign. Yes, give me a clear sign that this is what you want me to do." I just gave God, Grandmother and Grandfather, this ultimatum and, for a split second, I thought to myself: *Thank goodness the weather is clear!*

I wouldn't want lightning to strike me. No chance of that on this clear day.

As I stood there deepening my breath, hoarse from screaming, and with drying tears on my face, not one but two big, beautiful golden eagles majestically appeared, dancing in flight together. As they caught the updraft, they rose next to my deck and the rocks beyond. They were close enough that I could count the talons on their feet and make out the specific color and design of their feathers. I believed that I caught a glimpse of their piercing eyes. It was like taking a deep drink from a well of joy.

This scene of just one, let alone two, eagles flying within twelve feet of my upstairs windows and deck was not a common occurrence. These eagles were not looking for a meal, because their prey was down below in the canyon. These eagles were here for me. I looked up and shouted out again, "Okay, God, here is the deal. I will write my dissertation as long as this is really what I am supposed to do. Every morning I will get up at five a.m. I will look west out on the Continental Divide and if an eagle flies by, then I will go to my desk and write for three hours."

Then the most wondrous thing happened. Every day for the next three months, I got up and went to the window or stood out on the deck. Sure enough, an eagle, sometimes two, would soar by and I would proceed to my desk to write from 5:00 a.m. to 8:00 a.m. Some days, the writing flowed; other days, writing meant holding up my head as I stared at the computer and the view out of my window. Regardless of the number of pages or words, I dutifully sat at my desk and dared not rise from my chair until the three hours had passed.

Admittedly, I did get a little perturbed at these eagle guides. Having written for three hours, I would ascend the stairs, enjoying the beauty of the morning, and make my breakfast. Contentedly eating my morning meal and planning my workday, I thought, *What else would I do today?* My plan would be thwarted. *Oh, no, not you again!* The eagles with their gorgeous and powerful wings would swoop by the window. My eagle guides were not taking no for an answer; the eagles were not accepting any procrastination about accomplishing my current purpose in life. All right. Grabbing my mug of herbal tea, I would return to the office for another three hours of writing.

Every day, I grew more and more appreciative of my connection to these magnificent birds that came to inspire me to stay on the path and complete my doctoral dissertation. Their presence delivered an energy of unconditional love, support, and courage to help me heal my deepest fears that I was unworthy or not good enough to hold the highest academic degree.

My eagle guides came in direct connection to my conversation with God, Grandmother and Grandfather. And in three months, the complete draft of my doctoral dissertation was ready for my committee chair to review. The eagles miraculously held the space for me to write what I learned about visionary leadership behavior in YWCA women executives from forty-three countries.

The act of looking for inspiration in nature, or whatever arises up for you, is an essential step in committing to positive action for healing. You can learn to trust your inner spirit and your universal spiritual connection to all of nature as well as human beings: friends, foes, colleagues, bosses, and strangers.

When you are grounded in this spiritual awareness, then you know you are sacred—you and I are all One. Your ability and choice to be conscious in your journey creates the opportunity for you to choose positive actions that create and honor life. Joy and success are an inevitable part of the positive choices that you make.

One of the greatest joys is to be in search of one thing and to then discover something else unexpectedly. Creative, positive action is not trying to control everything with a tightly planned, rigid structure, which is one of the ways that we rob ourselves of the joy of living in right relationship to creation. Alice Walker said, "In search of my mother's garden, I found my own."[5] The pure joyfulness of the unexpected can continue to be a source of wonder.

The cycle of healing is a full process: listening, supportive relationships, unconditional love, and commitment to creative, positive action, again and again, covering all areas of the whole of you—physical, emotional, mental, and spiritual.

WHAT NEEDS HEALING IN OUR LIVES?

It's not true, but it almost seems as if human beings are condemned to get stuck in the suffering cycle. We see that pain happens at many levels: individual, family, community, nation, and world. Each of these pains needs and wants healing. It is a gift just to be aware that healing is needed and to avoid self-delusion, denial, or other barriers to reaching for happiness.

So many people suffer from alienation and depression. Even

in economically developed countries, the rates of depression continue to grow. Destruction of the environment, global warming, thoughtless governmental, business, and individual actions that harm the earth—all have consequences that injure each of us. The list of things that cry out for healing goes on and on, injustices of all kinds: unemployment, inadequate health care, destruction of culture, and loss of hope. Rather than addressing any of this, we try to dismiss or ignore the problem or blame someone.

Even our methods of healing are fragmented, separating and compartmentalizing our wholeness. When something is wrong, our initial reaction is often *I want to get rid of it, I want to kill it, I want things to go back to the way they used to be!*

The gift of healing can be more than that. It can go beyond fixing, beyond bouncing back from change or hurt. My mother and grandmother might enjoy a good movie where the heroine defeats and even kills the demons or the monsters. But when they shared with us their wisdom of the healing process and spoke about living as a whole human being, the journey was never about going out and finding devils or demons and killing them. The healing journey was always one of continually learning, listening to understand, and being the life-giving connection to yourself and to others.

We can transcend. We can go forward through healing and become part of a different journey, as my son did in healing his broken heart. He did not return to Alex, the twenty-year-old from before; he healed and transformed and expanded into the next phase of his life, a more conscious, expansive life he shares with the collective Universe. Through healing, he became someone more, someone new, and someone greater, a part of something greater than his circumstances. His spirit embraced his resilience.

My mother, drawing on her knowledge that we are all truly connected, always said, "The ultimate law and authority is love and kindness, and as you go through life, bring the darkness into the light." To make ends meet, she took care of many children on weekdays, in addition to my siblings and me. She was always good with the small children she babysat, kissing their hands and telling them they were beautiful, and taking such loving care of them.

Two of those children, a brother and sister, were four and five years old. They had been in a horrific house fire. Their melted faces hardly looked human. My mom would kiss each on the forehead, even more than the other children, loving that child and making them beam in happiness. I asked her how she could do this. I could read to them, but it was scary for me to touch them. She said, "Oh, but they're part of me and they're part of you."

Today, when I think of healing, it is a healing of all those different parts of the child within ourselves that we do not want to kiss. Great Spirit makes no mistakes: Part of our work in healing is learning self-love through how we treat others, who are ultimately the same and a part of us.

The people, earth, and spirit—the circle of life and abundant creation that we have been talking about are One. There can be no healing if we are always fighting off the demons of "us and them." We can bomb the world into pieces, and we can destroy parts of ourselves hoping to *get rid of that part.* But the truth is, we cannot bomb the world or destroy ourselves into peace and wholeness. We are all a part of each other. We all share this consciousness. We are one diverse family sharing this planet together.

I remember watching cowboy movies as a kid with my brothers and sisters. The lone cowboy, outnumbered, would hop on his horse and go out to fight. We thought: *That guy is crazy! This makes no sense. Wouldn't you go with your whole tribe? He is doomed. He needs to wake up. What is he doing?*

What are *we* doing? Are we choosing to fight? Or are we aiming to heal with the support of our relations? This journey of oneness is not a cliché. Oneness means we are all connected. We do not have power over anyone or anything. Human beings are not separate from the planet and cannot afford the illusion of being above concern. We do not, and could not, live alone, without all the other human beings, or without water, fish, animals, plants, oxygen, and the earth. We must remember that all these things, our relations, are part of our process of healing.

For so many years, I heard myself telling and retelling the story of being alone in my big hurt of abuse and violence, which is also a story for women around the world. My identity became attached to the story of my pain, making it so difficult to move beyond it to see what could be created. As I let go of the pain, I began to see glimmers of the possible love that I was meant to experience and share. In the process, I was better able to love and care for myself, and accept love and care from others.

As we experience this, we come to trust that there is a place beyond recovery, beyond what we think of as healing.

We discover our positive role in evolution, far more than just getting back to where we were. This is a knowing of our own sacredness, our spirit calling us into our wholeness to become something larger and more life-giving.

We have to stop looking at healing and recovery as we used to know it and use this gift of healing so that we look for transcendence. We are not going back to anything. We are using the original wisdom to release ourselves to new ways of being, of seeing, of living our connectedness.

We now have scientific proof that trauma survivors can change in profound ways beyond their pre-trauma baseline, growing beyond resilience to become even higher functioning as a result of their healing process. This is what original indigenous wisdom tells and what we observe in nature: Healing *is* a process, rarely a single event, and can result in greater wisdom and the willingness to risk being more fully alive—a whole human being.

You have the capacity for love, for giving, for creativity, for being able to call all of that forth; that is part of the original wisdom with which you can heal yourself and heal others—people, earth, and spirit. There is a light within you that can never be extinguished, even though you may lose sight of it in moments of suffering. It remains pure, almost like a child who asks by their very being: "Honor my sacredness."

HEALING OUR SPIRIT

Elders mostly teach us about "good medicine" and how we can stay focused on the state of being a healthy, whole human. This is a powerful lesson that we now apply in many aspects of our modern lives. However, in supporting us to live as whole human beings, they would be remiss if they did not tell us about "bad medicine."

The first and second of these bad medicines are bad thoughts and bad words. Elders state unequivocally that thoughts and words have power. As my Osage Elder told us kids when we were little: "If you think bad thoughts or speak bad words about yourself or others, you are harming people, earth, and spirit. You are using bad medicine."

These negative thoughts and words can limit our ability to create happiness in our lives and in the lives of those we touch. We know now, through neurophysiology and the use of medical imaging, that when we think bad thoughts, see threatening images, or experience bad emotions, our bodies release hormones to prepare us to protect ourselves. When too many of these hormones, such as cortisol, flood our bodies over time, we are susceptible to physiological stresses that can open us up to sickness.

Elders share that even if you are not the one to speak the bad words, you become a participant and are responsible simply by listening to it. Listening to bad medicine is in itself bad medicine, for it has an emotional, spiritual, and physical impact on you. Elders and healers maintain that by listening we give the bad medicine strength and perpetuate it.

The third form of bad medicine is dirty looks. These looks do damage not only to others but to ourselves. Nothing needs to be spoken, but one can always sense the negative intent of these nonverbal dirty looks. Regularly, my mother and my uncle instructed us to be kind and gentle and not to give dirty looks.

As Yankton Dakota and Chickasaw First Nation Elder Phil Lane Jr. said, "The hurt of one is the hurt of all. The honor of one is the honor of all."[6] In alignment with this knowledge, my mother and Elders taught that even when you are the recipient of bad medicine, you need to be kind and gentle. You never need to accept it; it denies dignity and respect to you and the other person, but you can try to understand and avoid creating more hurt in response. You have a choice: to perpetuate and intensify it, or to disarm it. These bad thoughts, bad words, and dirty looks are bad medicine that affect us all.

What do we do to heal from bad medicine? We actively don't engage in it, we move away from it, and we spread compassion for those who are using it.

Once, I was walking at the local outdoor mall with my young sons, Alex, then eight, and Nico, then three. An older boy said something to Alex as he passed him. I saw Alex was upset, his head and shoulders turned down, and he moved away from the older boy. Alex turned to me and said, "Mom, something bad happened to that boy. He said something really mean to me; something must have happened to him." Alex could feel it, sense it, and, in his young wisdom, had compassion for that boy.

It is never right to hurt or oppress anyone, no matter what gender, age, race, orientation, or physical challenges. We know

now that the actions that damage one human being damage all of us. We need to stop spreading the hurt and avoid creating more harm and areas to be healed.

Good medicine, by contrast, creates healing and is strengthened through following a spiritual practice. There is a broad diversity of powerful indigenous and non-indigenous spiritual practices available to us to create harmony. Those spiritual practices include meditation, ceremony, sweat lodges, prayer, chanting, dance, yoga, and acknowledgment of a higher conscious, such as Great Spirit, God, Allah, Holy Spirit, Universe, or cosmic energy within ourselves and between all of us.

They also include any of the ways in which you connect with nature, listening to the earth, the stars, the trees, all the plants, the rocks, the moon, the animals, and the elements. When you listen to the hearts of those around you and express gratitude for all that you have been given, you are engaging in one of the highest forms of good medicine.

The power of one is the power of all. The hurt of one is the hurt of all. The healing of one is the healing of all. Recognizing and acting in empathy, kindness, and love creates transcendence for all. All people's ancestors were once indigenous, and ultimately, if you choose to remember and practice the original wisdom of harmony and connection, you return to right relationship with all life.

During my first time at the Grand Canyon, a Navajo park ranger told us a story of the Rim Walker. He said the Rim Walker represents each of us, and as he walks the rim and begins his descent into the canyon, he is thinking about life and the responsibility for ourselves and for others, about our ability to harm and to heal. He is thinking of the grand connection between us. He stops at different points and is troubled. He thinks: *I thought I had healed this, I thought this was done.*

He looks out over the canyon, at its beauty and its depth, and is reminded that, *Yes, I did, but there is also another level, a deeper level, another part of remembering the wholeness. There is still more to learn about the sacred circle. I must simply keep walking to see it.*

Our journey continues, and as it does, we continue to heal others and ourselves.

Great spirit
Guide us to drum
To sing out our voices.

—MA-NEE CHACABY,
OJIBWA-CREE ELDER, CANADA

THE MEDICINE OF HEALING

You have the gift of healing with spirit. Healing does not have to be complicated; you can begin with your first locus of control, which is your breath. A simple powerful practice that you can consciously do for a few minutes and several times a day is to be aware of your breathing.

Inhale love and kindness, exhale love and kindness, inhale love and kindness, exhale love and kindness, again and again.

With this practice, we begin to reinforce that we are a part of an abundant world, one where healing and growth are natural and normal, where hurts can be prevented and, when they occur, those hurts can be healed, starting from within.

To anchor this healing medicine further, you can create a measurable goal to be healthy and vital. Once you have identified your goal for health and vitality, then I've found that affirmations said multiple times a day support you in being good medicine in the world to yourself and to others.

Please create a healthy goal for your life followed by healing affirmations for yourself. A present-tense affirmation written in the "I" voice with action words will help create a potent affirmation of the desired result of healing, vitality, and wholeness. For example, my lifelong adult affirmation is: "I am so happy and grateful discovering and trusting my gifts so that I can be a life-giving connection to all."

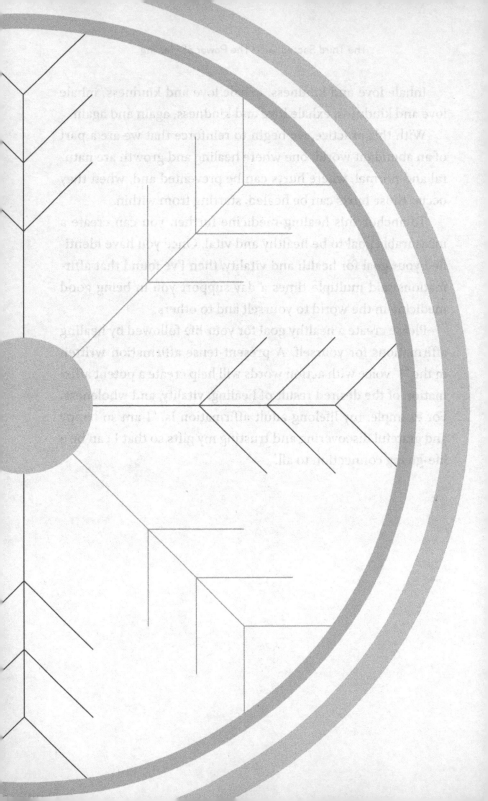

6

The Fourth Sacred Gift: The Power of Hope

More than ever, we need to remember that the earth is our Mother . . . By talking to Mother Earth, by being with her, by giving thanks to her. By crying to her when we need her nourishment. As long as we learn again and practice again, to have a good relationship with Mother Earth, there is hope that we may continue being here.

—ARKAN LUSHWALA, AN INDIGENOUS PERUVIAN SPIRITUAL LEADER

FROM OUR HOUSE WITH its fresh green paint, shiny-smooth wood floors, and huge windowpanes, we can look out in every direction at the Colorado blue skies dotted with billowy white clouds ascending from the tops of the evergreens. Thirteen of us, family and friends, are sitting in a circle of chairs in anticipation of the start of the Blessing Way Ceremony for my twenty-month-old son, Nico. In the center of our circle rests the morning star quilt, a gift from Norbert Hill of the Oneida tribe to my son.

The morning star quilt is one of the most valued gifts of the Northern Plains Indians given to honor a special friend, a newly married couple, or to parents in celebration of a child's birth. The handmade quilt is six feet by six feet, and in the center is a four-and-one-half-foot, richly colored, eight-pointed morning star made from a quilt pattern of yellow, gold, orange, brown, and black pieces of fabric. The eight-pointed star symbolizes hope and guidance. The brightest morning star, which is actually Venus, stands between darkness (ignorance) and light (knowledge), showing us the power of hope, an understanding that a new day is dawning.

We settle down and become still. Then Eddie Bent Box Sr., the seventy-eight-year-old Southern Ute Elder, stands and signals to my six-year-old son, Alex, to sit on his left and assist him. Alex smiles at the Elder and quickly runs over to assume his place. Eddie says, "I am wearing my eagle-feathered headdress, tribal clothes, and handmade beaded moccasins. Each time I put these on, I stand taller." His eyes twinkle and he shows a slight playful smile, for he is maybe five feet two inches tall.

"After I finished my service in the U.S. Navy in the South Pacific through World War II, I then began to follow the spiritual path of my grandfathers by entering the Ute Indian Sundance. At the personal level, a dancer must receive a command, which often comes to him through a dream. You must abstain from both food and liquid and undergo various ceremonies inside the Sundance lodge. I danced for days, moved by the drumming and singing. This is spiritual for us individual dancers, a quest for spiritual power and purification: We are in direct communion with the Great Spirit.

"The medicine power is strictly individual. Each time you have to reckon with the spiritual world by yourself and cope with the long days and nights and the pains of the spiritual quest alone. When you get the medicine power, you can choose to use or abuse it. However, there is a community aspect of the Sundance: We participate as members of a family, who pitch their tipi around the edge of the Sundance grounds to support you vigorously, both spiritually and physically, in singing, drumming, or silence."

Eddie looks around the circle and continues. "The presence of the family is absolutely crucial in giving the Sundancer strength and sustenance as he undergoes his quest. Although we are there on our own and the medicine power is for each dancer's own use, the power is ultimately not the individual's at all. The medicine power comes from the ultimate source, the Great Spirit, and is given for a purpose: to be used in service to your family and community.

"The Sundancer becomes the instrument via which the family and my entire Ute community attempts to achieve spiritual rejuvenation and reinforce the common spiritual power which has traditionally served to bind us together. And so long as the Sundance tradition persists, and so long as the Sundancers receive their dream vision and come forward to dance, the survival of the people is assured."

We all were in awe as we saw, behind Eddie, two eagles fly by the windows.

"From 1956 to 1994, I was asked to lead this most sacred

ceremony, the Sundance of the Ute People. I tell you this for we must not take lightly any of the different ceremonies that the Great Spirit has given to us. Today we are witness to young Nico's blessing with the Great Spirit, which requires us to follow the instructions."

Eddie tells me to take off Nico's shirt and hold him in my arms. As I stand in the center of the circle holding Nico, what strikes me most is Eddie's wise, loving face and eyes framed by the full white-and-brown eagle-feathered headdress. He then shares some prayers and songs in his Ute language.

Our family and friends watch as Eddie and Nico, without blinking, lock eyes with each other. Their eyes sparkle. Solemnly, the Elder opens a small tobacco can that contains red powdery earth from his tribe's sacred lands. Before he can begin to paint Nico's body with this sacred earth, Nico places his two pudgy little fingers into the canister, carefully takes the earth, and makes deliberate marks: first across his chest, then on his arms, and finally, on his face in patterns that bring a huge smile to the Elder. Eddie tells us, "Each tribe has its own designs and paints for their bodies and faces for rituals, dances, and for battle. Young Nico has just drawn some of those designs on his body."

Eddie closes the canister and Nico gets down from my arms, and they nod to each other. Eddie reaches into his bag, brings out a ceremonial flute, and says, "Nico, this is yours. The little beaded turtle at this end of the flute is you, and the red cardinal bird at the other end will watch over you, the little turtle, as you grow."

As Nico looks at the flute, Eddie explains to us, "The turtle is a sacred symbol: It represents Mother Earth, it signifies good health and long life for Nico. And the red cardinal bird knows that everything that he does is of importance, and with the cardinal's distinct loud and clear whistle, the bird will remind Nico to listen closely and pay attention to his creativity and intuition of what is right, always."

Then Nico smiles and, taking the beautifully carved brown wooden flute, places his lips on it and plays, his fingers moving up and down, closing and opening various holes. After about ten seconds of playing, he carefully places the flute down next to his older brother, Alex. The Elder returns to his chair next to Alex and begins to beat the drum and chant.

Nico begins to dance, using all the space in the center of the circle—not like the way a two-year-old dances when watching children's videos or listening to music on the stereo. Instead, Nico instinctively dances in movements that seem ancient and steady, a ceremonial dance of the Blessing Way.

The silent circle of family and friends watches this timeless connection between the Elder, the child, and this spiritual ceremony, which carries all the hope, wisdom, and joy that have been a part of life for countless generations. The blessing ceremony also projects all this hope and spiritual strength into the future, for the generations to come.

My six-year-old son asks the Elder, "How does Nico know what to do?"

Eddie replies, "The relations are with him and they are with you, too. It is easy to remember, if you wish it. It is easy to dance, if you wish it. It is important to not forget. It is life. It is the circle."

As my little twenty-month-old son dances freely, open to every sound, every energy, I am transported to a time when I was much younger, closer to his innocent age. I allow my memories to take over and recall the time when I was that toddler dancing, dancing at the gatherings with my beautiful *mestizo* mix of Mexican and Aztecan family.

I am filled with a sense of everything being as it should be, as it is meant to be, and I am filled with peace, joy, and hope. But then my eyes fill with tears as I recall a dark memory, when I forgot the sacredness of the dance of life.

I was thirteen when my father was murdered. And with his tragic death, the drunken anger and sexual abuse stopped. I no longer had to live in fear, but the horrible images and memories of abuse plagued me.

I was in one of my worst moments, drowning in memories and feelings of shame, fear, and pain. I couldn't live this way anymore, and I decided one afternoon, a few months after my father's murder, to end my life.

I went to the kitchen, climbed on a chair, and stepped onto the yellow Formica countertop so I could reach the highest kitchen cabinet. This was where my mother stored the medicine, to keep it out of the reach of the children.

As I searched I thought: *No, not her heart medicine: too expensive to use that.* Then I grabbed a large bottle of aspirin. I quickly took the bottle and carried it upstairs to the bedroom I shared with my two sisters. I closed the door and, gulping water, quickly began to swallow the pills. I imagined myself going to sleep; however, this sleep would not include any beautiful dreams. Rather, this sleep would put an end to the horrible images of my dad and me. *But what if I get sick? I don't want my sisters to have to clean up after me.* I moved the trash can next to me.

My body started shaking and I moved the trash can closer. I began to throw up violently. The door was no barrier to the sounds. Soon my bed was surrounded by my sisters, brothers, and my mom. I heard my mother's voice, as if in the distance, saying, "What were you thinking? You are not to die! There has been enough death in this house. I'm taking you to the bishop!"

I did not know how the bishop could stop the horrible pain, but I now knew for certain that I did not want to die. I was so grateful to have my family around me. As I continued to shake and throw up, I begged the spirits: *Oh, please, please, let me get through the pain. I want to live; I am supposed to be here in the circle with my three brothers, my two sisters, and my mom.*

As my body continued to expel the aspirin, I drifted from the pain as I internally sensed the loving touch of my grandmother's soft, wrinkled hand as we walked to the green vegetable garden in her backyard. I could feel the warmth of the dark, rich dirt over my hands as she helped me plant a flower seed, a *mirasol.* I could then see my toddler's rocking chair in the corner of the bedroom, a special gift from my grandfather. These loving images guided me out of my pain, giving me the courage to wake up and be with my family; they reminded me that I am an important part of this family.

And it is this power of family and community that brings me back to the present—to the Blessing Way and the sound of the drums' rhythmic heartbeat, and the smiles of the circle of my family and friends. I found myself back in the room with the Ute Elder Eddie Box, watching the innocent dance of my little Nico.

Most of us have had feelings of hopelessness at some time or other; this is a normal part of life. Joy and sorrow, hope and doubt, light and darkness, can and do coexist. No matter what your circumstance today, no matter how bad things can get, you will eventually find that everything eventually changes.

Humans have a way of believing, in our minds, that the experience of the past, or of this moment, will last forever. That is not the case. Life's troubles do not have a life of their own; they are not permanent unless we decide to make them permanent. Knowing this, we can look with hope to the future and sit, stand, or even dance like crazy during life's journey, filled with wise joy, like little Nico. We are always a part of the circle of life; we will always have the dance within us, if we recall our place in the circle.

As I sat in the Blessing Way Ceremony, watching my son dancing to the Elder's drums and chants, despite what had happened in the past, I know the power of connection and love—of hope. I am part of the mystery and the dance of life. I invite *you* to remember the dance, your dance, our dance, and to participate.

Become aware of what gives you hope, which actions create the power and the gift of hope. Remember, the power of hope is not an illusion, an amorphous thing. Hope is a constant and dependable source of energy.

WHAT IS HOPE?

Hope is an energy source. It may not be understood by modern science, but indigenous people and many others have an inner certainty that there is something bigger than any one of us. People call this greater source for hope by many names: Grandmother and Grandfather, God, Allah, Universe, Tao, cosmic energy, nature, consciousness, or original wisdom. For everyone, and under whatever label or banner it resides, it represents the connection between people, earth, and spirit.

When we open ourselves to hope, it is possible to release the pressure and desire to know everything, the need to think we are in control. It is, in fact, impossible to know all the answers. There is no certainty. Any control we think we have is an illusion. But hope, this infinite energy source, can inspire us, and can help pull us through even the most difficult times as they arise in our lives.

Through the Internet and media, we continuously are made aware of the realities of economic disparity, colonization, war, violence and terror, environmental degradation, and desperation worldwide. We can see the scars that all of that has left behind, in societies, in the landscape, in the earth we walk on, and in the rivers, lakes, and oceans that sustain us.

We can see the pain and the devastation and displacement of people and cultures throughout the world. Yet the gift of hope fortifies us to see the problems and to choose to focus on what is working, to sidestep discouragement and despair. We can choose to embrace the real possibility that together, through our individual and collective action, we can make things not only better but as they are intended to be, a reflection of the abundance.

As Wangari Maathai said in a speech after receiving the 2004 Nobel Peace Prize: "In the course of history, there comes a time when humanity is called to shift to a new level of consciousness, to reach a higher moral ground. A time when we have to shed our fear and give hope to each other. That time is now."[7]

Indeed, the time is now. We must use this energy source, the gift of hope, to imagine something better and to take positive individual and collective action.

THE DANGER OF DOUBT

Limiting beliefs—conscious and unconscious—and our interpretation of events can lead us to believe that there is no hope. The belief in the story we tell ourselves that no real future is possible can become a paralysis, stopping us from being and doing what is ours to be and do.

There is a reason that you are here. Of all the beings that could be here, it is you and me; all of us have been called here at this time. There are indigenous principles cautioning you about what you think or what you say, because all thoughts and actions have an impact. But there is also much celebration and expectation: Hope and action can shift our conscious- and unconscious-limiting beliefs and allow us to release and transcend them.

As Chief Oren Lyons says, "A leader never takes away the hope of the people."[8] In fact, it was the hopelessness I felt as a thirteen-year-old that caused me to take that bottle of aspirin, forgetting the sacred connection that has been and always will be mine.

I have heard many stories of hope and of hopelessness in my work, including when I am facilitating the building of effective cross-cultural teams and leaders in business. A common theme and description of hopelessness is the doubt that provokes it.

Doubt, an uncertain or undecided frame of mind, creeps in, calling into question actions that can make a new dream or vision come true. The doubt can come from someone's skeptical look or words. Or it can come from a voice inside yourself, the internal critic that says your dream or idea is absurd, or that you are not good enough to achieve your dream.

People's fear of uncertainty, risk, or possible failure is a killer of the drive to create positive change. Even though the current state may not be comfortable, it is familiar, so doubt dashes the desire and hope for creating something new and better. When doubt is allowed to take center stage, the status quo prevails and hope can die right there.

On the other hand, I have also heard women and men share some common themes of how they have a vision, a hopeful dream, and they have actually welcomed the doubt that inevitably comes along during the journey to fulfill that dream. They view the doubt as a strength-builder, as they've learned to ask for help from others and to trust in things known and unknown, which has been a tremendous positive force in their endeavors.

As you may recall, when I first received the four sacred gifts from my Elders, I spoke to one of the Elders, Henrietta. I asked,

"I still do not have all the answers to my question, do I?" My question was one filled with doubt about my higher purpose, and whether I had the power to make a real difference in the world.

Henrietta said, "Anita, you think that the worst thing that has ever happened to our people was our being murdered and having our sacred lands taken? You are wrong. The worst thing that can happen to our people, or to any people, is to lose hope."

Her words were like lightning striking my heart and soul. It was then I knew what my purpose was, why I was there to receive the four sacred gifts; the gifts were the perfect answer to my question. They gave me the strength now to take action and fulfill my dreams.

JASMIN'S JOURNEY: THE POWER
OF HOPE IN ACTION

A businesswoman, Jasmin epitomizes and embodies the gift of hope. She is a Torres Strait Islander by birth who lives in Australia and who, like many Aboriginal and Torres Strait Island people, has suffered mistreatment to herself, her family, and her ancestors as a result of colonization and the mindsets and structures that perpetuate dehumanization. She does not accept that indigenous people are not supposed to dream, that they should forget the dreams of their ancestors, so she creates businesses providing employment, pride, and products with an Indigenous instinct.

When Jasmin was online at the OfficeMax Australia site

buying schoolbooks for her children, she realized there were few books to be found about her culture. She decided that it didn't have to be this way; she had hope for something better.

Through her determination—despite her color and her class, despite bureaucracy and its built-in obstacles—she made her way to the executive offices of the OfficeMax Australia corporation. Perhaps initially out of politeness, an executive listened to her story and replied, "Well, I'm not exactly sure of what you want. Why don't you bring us a business proposal?" In a matter of days, Jasmin formed a business plan to sell indigenous-branded stationery under the name Tjindgarmi. Tjindgarmi, a Torres Strait Island warrior, is a fictional creation of Jasmin's imagination written for her children to introduce all the things she discovered and loved about her culture: the beauty of Torres Strait pearls, the island stone fish traps, the abundant food source of the sea, and the wisdom of myths, particularly of the octopus and the tiger shark, which is her island's totem.

Thus began in 2014 this relationship between OfficeMax Australia and Jasmin. However, the story continues, for now they both get excited about the expansive possibility to partner on and present educational materials about indigenous people's history, knowledge, and contributions to Australia.

With an open heart, Jasmin writes a story of a young girl, Teter Mek, a Torres Straits Islander, who is washed out to sea in a storm surge. The young girl drifts for days. Suffering from amnesia and near death, she is rescued by a fisherman in an old boat. Teter Mek begins a journey of self-discovery, trying to find out who she is and where her parents have gone. During her travels, which take her to towns and cities throughout Australia, she hears many inspiring stories from different Aboriginal people and Torres Straits Islanders. Her journey highlights the connection of these different indigenous people with country and community.

The Teter Mek story becomes an educational school initiative that includes storybooks, lesson plans, and workbooks accompanied by art and handcrafted merchandise to be rolled out in schools in 2017. Jasmin proposes that she and OfficeMax together offer this curriculum to the children and people of Australia to tell of the contributions, both past and ongoing, of the country's first people, and she creates the Teter Mek Foundation to use some of the proceeds of the Tjindgarmi product sales to fund education and promote confidence and pride for her indigenous people.

Jasmin did not get bogged down with bad news; she used hope to feed her awareness, vision, and collective action, working with family and new executive allies within Office-Max. Together they have created a beautiful, broad initiative to share information about the culture, traditions, and wisdom of indigenous people through the stores of the largest seller of textbooks across Australia. The business partnership between Jasmin's Tjindgarmi business products, her nonprofit Teter Mek Foundation, and OfficeMax Australia is a concrete result of hope in action.

Hope is a spiritual muscle. It is a practice, one in which vision and dreams play a critical part. Hope in action bridges the ordinary—what can be seen and known—with the extraordinary world of what one imagines. It is the miraculous light of the baby doll in my dreams, and the adult at nineteen, who re-experienced the forever-light and now knows it on a daily basis.

Acting with this hope, acting with faith, acting with the knowledge of something unproven is a powerful energy that helps us live as whole human beings. Hope in action is an act of freedom. It is an antidote to the doubt and the pain existing in the world around us. Václav Havel speaks of the power of hope:

> The kind of hope that I often think about, . . . I understand above all as a state of mind, not a state of the world. Either we have hope within us or we don't. It is a dimension of the soul. . . . Hope is not prognostication. It is an orientation of the spirit, an orientation of the heart; it transcends the world that is immediately experienced, and is anchored somewhere beyond its horizons. . . . Hope is not the conviction that something will turn out well, but the certainty that something makes sense regardless of how it turns out.[9]

INDIVIDUAL AND COLLECTIVE HOPE

What does it take to develop and sustain hope? What does it take to trust in your vision, to honor the action that demonstrates that, in connection, abundance exists? We return to the indigenous worldview: the circle of connection between people, earth, and spirit.

We can allow ourselves to be nourished by the energy of hope. We can create something from its radiant light. Hope can cause things to change at the speed of your imagination. Hope can provide the inspiration and vision that allow you to see what might be possible along the wonderful and sometimes challenging journey to achieve it.

Hope draws you toward itself and then invites your efforts to bring it about. Some call this space between what you hope for and what the current reality is a "gap." This is not a gap of nothingness; it is the structural tension that draws your mind, body, and spirit to trust and move toward what is hoped for. What sustains hope is the act of looking for and seeing signs of hope becoming realized. This requires a positive outlook. With this practice, more of your energy is used to see what is working and what is possible than is spent focusing on the problems. It replaces the habit of constant use of negative thoughts and non-generative words and images that cause tunnel vision, preventing us from sensing all the possibilities.

Instead of seeing only the things that are not working, give more focus, more of your energy, more of your light, and more of your mind to what is working inside of yourself and outside in the world. Take time to have fun, share laughter, dance, and engage in positive conversations with others. Search out the movements, organizations, and people who give you hope, such as those who study and mimic the extraordinary design of nature to create answers to problems that seem insurmountable. Create a world that works for all of us.

Individuals and groups are awakening to a new way of business and community, focusing on creating work and community environments that invite us to include our passion and joy, which is what a sustainable world needs. And this process of action is a vaccination against despair and apathy. For example, take the conscious business movements or environmental movements that define and measure success by creating a sustainable world. These include people and organizations that focus on repairing the damage that has been done and creating harmonious development, giving holistic consideration to care for people and for our Mother Earth, for this and future generations.

As you draw in hope, you reflect it back to your community. It becomes a positive cycle within the circle of oneness, benefiting all our precious relations. Surround yourself with people, nature, and images that support hope-filled action. What you focus on creates the conditions for positive possibilities and change.

THE WINDS OF CHANGE

I'm thirty-two. I open the large wooden door of the brick building where I have entered many times, taking classes and exams. There are eight other doctoral students present; to each I give a brief smile and then go take a seat at a large table.

I'm filled with anticipation regarding the quality of my written responses to a series of questions, which will determine whether I have a green light to become a doctoral candidate. In order to receive the title of doctoral candidate, I must submit a doctoral dissertation on a researchable topic bringing new knowledge to the field. My field of study is organizational development connected to behavioral and social sciences—basically, how human systems work.

With sweaty palms I take the paper from the professor, glance at the questions, and begin my day of exams. A week later, the results are posted on the department's wall: Two of us have passed and carry the designation of doctoral candidate. With a deep sigh of relief, I'm positively ecstatic, feeling affirmed as having a sound theoretical knowledge base to now enter the final phase, presenting my doctoral dissertation in writing and an oral defense.

With scientific studies, theory, and practice in hand, I begin the arduous process of working with my committee to support my dissertation question, which is about the contribution of personality temperament and organizational variables to visionary leadership behavior. With great pride, I include the stories and quotes of indigenous Elders who were great visionary leaders: Black Elk, Chief Sitting Bull, and others. Their knowledge sits right beside my acknowledgment of works from Harvard professors who study leadership.

Therefore, I am quite confused at first when I hear different members of my doctoral committee say, "No, you must take out the indigenous Elders, their stories and experiences. You are doing grounded science and these stories are anecdotal, not tested science."

I retort, "Indigenous people have been doing sound science for thousands of years. Science is about knowledge, the systematic study of the world based on facts learned through experiments and observations." I feel myself taking a deep breath and continue: "Indigenous science and practice are not anecdotal. These Elders and our people have survived for millennia based on reliable accounts of the real world. Testing and retesting through observation and experience has given us a deep understanding of the natural world and our interconnections."

My heart is pounding, for I can sense threat, that I am being told to separate my cultural scientific understanding of the world and what is modern science in order to continue my dissertation.

For a moment my body and spirit leave this conversation and I imagine myself in a different university office that houses the American Indian Science and Engineering Society. The director, Norbert Hill, PhD, of the Oneida tribe, and Vine Deloria Jr., PhD, brilliant Standing Rock Sioux professor, are talking with students, alumni, and friends.

I hear Professor Deloria speak of the ways in which our ancestors, our people, have survived by using the original wisdom passed down to us from our Elders through observation and experience. He says that even though scientists are not acknowledging the wisdom of our Elders, scientific findings are often corroborating our experience and knowledge.

I am pulled back to my conversation when one doctoral committee member says, "Anita, you cannot get the highest degree in this country by not following the protocols. I understand your passion. And I acknowledge there is indigenous wisdom. Take these sections out and after you get your PhD, then you can write and speak about whatever you want. Bring all of this indigenous science into your work and into your contributions to the world." He looks down at his papers, which signals to me to leave. I immediately go to the chair of my committee and make my case for citing indigenous leaders and he says words to the same effect: "Take it out and after you get your degree, then you can study what you want."

As I leave his office, I am transported for a moment to my childhood. I am coming home from school and sharing with my mom what I am studying. I tell her that they are teaching us that George Washington was the first leader of our country, but this is not what our indigenous Elders are teaching us. My mom continues cooking and says in a loving, clear voice, "Anita, if you want to get an A, then you answer the way they want you to answer out there. But know that you can always come home and we can talk about the truth."

I respond, "But, Mom . . ."

My mom continues: "Anita, you get to choose. And remember, the winds are always changing, and someday the wind will be at our backs and we will be able to speak the truth and create change that we have always dreamt of."

Spending days considering my doctoral committee member's and committee chair's words, I know that they have always wanted my success. I reluctantly choose to do what I am told and take out the citations about indigenous Elders and their wisdom. In that moment, my fear that I would be denied my doctorate overcomes my commitment to honoring the wisdom of my Elders. With this decision, it feels like I am cutting off one of my arms. It will take time to reattach it and heal the wound.

When we lose hope, we need to engage in action that rebalances our sense of wholeness. In taking action, we invest in a vision of what we hope to see, know, and experience. We shift into creating what we yearn for, and in doing so, we revitalize our capacity to hope.

I have revisited that doctoral decision to drop the naming of my visionary Elders often, and have spoken about it in public on several occasions. In doing so, I am holding myself and my difficult decision, made in fear, with compassion and understanding. As I engage in this healing, I am speaking my truth and taking a stand for what I truly believe. I am replenishing my hope through action.

In all the years since that day, working with women and men around the world, I have committed to listening and learning from their different perspectives. I have learned that when I hold space for others to speak their truth, whatever it is, without judgment, I affirm the truth of all our experiences. With this open heart, I am able to imagine new possibilities and engage in hope-filled, positive action. We provide a mirror of hope for each other when we are truly present, learning from the past but not living there.

Today is an entirely new day! I can look to the east and see the morning star. The winds of change are blowing. Yes, there are those people who still do not acknowledge indigenous science. However, this illusion of separateness is dissipating, mending, and being sewn back together. We are rediscovering what indigenous Elders have always known: the essential connections that exist between all people and the earth. In the course of our busy modern lives, we each may have cut off parts of our inner knowing, losing connection to our truth and the wisdom of our spirit. Still, we each have the power to regain our wholeness. We can gaze inside, seeing the places where our spirit has withered from compromise, neglect, and fear, and we can enrich that soil, bringing water and light to let those flowers bloom again. We know what our heart desires; our work is to truly listen and feed the best of our spirit.

LIGHTING AND KEEPING THE FIRES LIT

The collective journey, your journey, and my journey all matter. You can keep the fires of hope lit by embracing your dreams and encouraging your visions. You can ask for dreams that will keep the flames from going out—dreams that can last a lifetime. You can let old stories die so that new dreams can be born.

Sometimes hope means believing in your childhood wisdom. It is often quickly labeled by others as naïveté, but actually it is clarity. Unmarred by limiting beliefs and experiences, your true strength may be this childhood knowing of who you really are—part of the miraculous, abundant world. Turn to the infant or toddler within you to be reminded that the sacred part of you is untouchable. Celebrate that bright spark of spirit within you. I now know this bright spark is the true me, no matter what abuse I endured during nine years of my childhood, and in spite of the gender, race, and economic systemic discrimination I have encountered as an adult. If you come upon a time when your hope is dimming, call on the wisdom of your brilliant child self. Invite that bright soul into your consciousness and ask them to give you the gift of their clear insight, refilling your well of innate intelligence and faith in the future. Listen, take it in, and thank them for their constant support for you. Now, sometimes, it so happens that you find the child is not the one to be your guide. If that is the case, then ask, gently, for your elder self, that wise manifestation of who you will become, to appear to you and offer perspective to replenish your hope. Knowing this older self is always there, you can feel confident of their caring and guidance. Thank them and, like the child, you can invite them to stay with you as you go through your day.

Another way to keep the fires of hope lit is to recognize the distinction between loneliness and being alone. Most of us have experienced loneliness, and yet, in closer review, we are never alone. We always have the natural world and animals around us. Even in the most desolate environments, torn by war and pollution, people connect to the warmth of the sun and a gentle breeze. And the outdoors, nature, always freely provides hope. It is wonderful just to smell the green grass, sit under a tree, listen to a bird singing, and, most of all, be able to walk barefoot on the sacred earth, knowing we do so with the spirit of our ancestors. So make time every day to really be present with the natural world, allowing the earth and all our relations to give you the deep and beautiful perspective that you are not alone, that they support you, your dreams, and your hopes.

And we have grandparents, relatives, and ancestors with us—those who are alive and those who have passed. We can call on their care, their love, and the memory and traditions of our ancestors to teach us, to remind us, of the joy of living as a whole human being. My practice, which I encourage you to try, is, as you lie down to go to sleep, ask your ancestors for advice, wisdom, and insight into whatever hopes, possibilities, challenges, or troubles are facing you. Then let go and slip into restful sleep, confident that you will get what you truly need when you awake (which may be something different from what you expected, such as the peaceful sleep your body and spirit needed). Before you arise, take time to give gratitude to spirit and ancestors for your sleep and for your transition to your awakening to a new day.

When we are consciously connecting with others around us, we are actually in ceremony, in a life-giving dance with them. One of the most wonderful ways that you can kindle hope is through action, meaningful service, and work done for and in the community. Build relationships in community, volunteer your gifts, become a caring member of your neighborhood. All these create and help sustain hope. We are spirit, energy in human form. Being together, engaged in action, is a form of ceremony that expands our happiness and creativity and inspires hope.

These are the four gifts: the power to forgive the unforgivable, the power of unity, the power of healing, and the power of hope. These four gifts were given to us from the Elders and from spirit to help us live as whole human beings, conscious of the impact our individual and collective thoughts and actions have on all our relations. We are part of, not separate from, the circle of people, earth, and spirit.

Since receiving the four gifts in 1995, I have worked diligently to apply what I learned to all parts of my life: my family; my work with leaders in business, government, and communities; and myself. Sometimes we do not get to see the results of our hopeful actions. When we do, it revives our belief that we can and do make a difference.

Fast-forward to 2007. I was anticipating my first journey to the sacred headwaters of the Amazon rain forest in Ecuador. This was a journey organized through the Pachamama Alliance, a nonprofit whose mission is to inspire people to create an environmentally sustainable, spiritually fulfilling, and socially just human presence on our planet. Their work in the Ecuador rain forest is to protect the rain forest by supporting the Achuar and other tribes, indigenous people who are the natural custodians of the forest.

As you can imagine, there was a lot of preparation for us on this journey: special equipment and clothes, inoculations, and conference calls full of planning. We immersed ourselves in the history, culture, ceremonies, and stories of the Achuar people and their environment through every book we could find. One day, while reading Joe Kane's book *Savages*, I read a certain passage and my eyes filled with tears. I shouted at my husband, "Kit, come here, you've got to read this!"

My husband responded, "Anita, it's a book, relax."

"But it is about our life and the Achuar, who we have not even met yet!"

I began to read aloud a passage that dated to 1990: "'DuPont's [CEO] Edgar Woolard had made it known that he would not give Conoco [a subsidiary of DuPont] the go-ahead for its Oriente [Ecuador Amazon basin] project unless the oil company came up with some sort of green blessing—some stamp of approval from the nonprofit community. Though Conoco had already invested $90 million, DuPont had to weigh these sums against the cost of being branded as trampling on the rights of, and quite possibly destroying, rain forest natives.'"[10]

Kit, eager for the news, asked, "Okay, how did it all turn out?"

I told him about a meeting described in the book between the native people and the oil company, and then continued to read aloud: "'Conoco announced it was pulling out of the Oriente. It would concentrate its energies about as far away from the Amazon as it could, the oil fields of Siberia.'"[11]

We breathed a great sigh of relief and wondered if our work with DuPont in the 1980s had played any part in this decision. In our work with executives and leaders of both Conoco and DuPont, our role as organizational consultants was to educate leaders and employees about multicultural awareness; their employee, customer, and worldwide diversity; and the value of respecting and learning from different cultures, people, and beliefs. I had specifically discussed the historic mistreatment of indigenous peoples, how governments and companies refused to consult, negotiate, and establish enforceable contracts that respected the dignity and basic human rights of tribal peoples around the world. Could it be that this work of ours had had an influence that became a part of their decision in 1990?

I thought to myself: *Life is miraculous!* Now, in 2007, seventeen years after the CEO of DuPont decided not to drill for oil in Ecuador, we would meet, face-to-face, with the very tribal people whose lives and lands were saved from drilling.

I believe that the Achuar probably already knew that Kit and I, in intuitive alignment with their people, had been working on their behalf and for life itself. Here was evidence that we are and were and have been all connected. I felt so fortunate to be shown this. I knew then that the story of the ancient tribes in the rain forests of Ecuador was my story, too.

Each of us has magical moments in our lives: moments when we become awakened to the oneness of all things; moments when we experience being part of the circle of life, no longer alone or separate. At these moments we are shown that the indigenous worldview is true, that even thousands of miles apart we are connected, impacting each other. We draw on the gift of hope when we learn to trust our own perceptions and experiences and our collective perceptions and experiences.

We understand it and embody it by listening to each other and through living our earthly as well as spiritual purpose in a conscious way. We discover that we have a relationship with the process of the universe that cannot be severed. Hope lives in us as we come to know that we are all connected and always will be.

Oh God, please hear our prayer
And give us your blessings.

—SEIKYO WAKE, JAPANESE ELDER
AND SHINTO PRIEST

THE MEDICINE OF HOPE

To reinforce my hopeful attitude, which guides my positive actions, each morning and each evening I sing a chant of gratitude to the Great Mystery. Recall that the Great Mystery is an indigenous way of standing in our connection with all beings that comes from spirit and from observation of people and nature. The Great Mystery is sometimes called Great Spirit; it is a concept of universal spiritual force providing hope in things seen and unseen.

I sing gratitude to the Great Mystery while imagining the winds of the four directions: east, south, west, and north. The winds remind us of our connection as they move around the earth, touching and connecting everyone and everything.

Please join me in singing this chant, and I invite you to sing it in your own native language:

Facing the East, sing:

It is said, it is said: Thank you, thank you, Great Mystery. Thank you. Thank you, Great Mystery.

Facing the South, sing:

It is said, it is said: Thank you, thank you, Great Mystery. Thank you. Thank you, Great Mystery.

Facing the West, sing:

It is said, it is said: Thank you, thank you, Great Mystery.
Thank you. Thank you, Great Mystery.

Facing the North, sing:

It is said, it is said: Thank you, thank you, Great Mystery.
Thank you. Thank you, Great Mystery.

Conclusion:
Nosotros Somos los Unos,
We Are the Ones

*We are not, and can never be, lone individuals. We are
the sum total of our actions as a species, and this is why
we can leave nobody out. We, as a species, holding one
part of the Hoop of Life, are responsible for upholding that
part. If we do not, the Hoop begins to fail. The Hoop of Life
does not understand "us and them," the Hoop of Life only
understands "We."*

—PAT MCCABE, NAVAJO ELDER

I CAN STILL FEEL the excitement and eagerness as we
prepare to visit my grandparents. No matter how often we
go, it is always a special occasion. My maternal grandparents
are the Medinas, and their home is the gathering place for the
family each Sunday and, if we are lucky, Saturdays, too! It is the
place where my grandparents weave together the Mexican way

and the indigenous Aztecan ways, telling us stories and loving us unconditionally.

My mom is the second oldest of ten children, three girls and seven boys. I love seeing her at Grandma's house. Whenever she returns to the home of her parents, she smiles more, and I can see her relax. Her smile and lighter spirit remind me that it is okay to consider this my other home, too, and that I belong to a larger family and community. It is a home filled with unbounded love and respect—a safe haven when I most need it.

These qualities are much greater and more important than any hardship, economic or otherwise. Life's intermittent pains are merely short disruptions to the main, happy event that is always taking place at my grandparents' house, reminding me of what is truly important in life: family and love.

My short *mestiza* grandmother was born on June 22, 1891, in San Francisco del Rincón, Mexico, to parents of Mexican and Aztec heritage. She is serious yet happy. I could tell this from her many smiles. Her face is broad, with prominent indigenous cheekbones, and her long silver hair is always tied up in a bun.

Grandma speaks Spanish and very little English, while my Spanish is nonexistent; my mother acts as translator. Even though we did not have long conversations, we learned to communicate without words. Her eyes and face would reflect her feelings, and she made soft, loving sounds that communicated her happiness and approval, or her slight and infrequent, often faint disapproval.

My grandparents respect the traditional ways, including

hard work, love for one's immediate and extended family, the importance of healing plants, and honoring the mystery of the healers and shamans—the indigenous *curanderos* (healers) of Mexico. My grandparents recognize the power of spirit in everything and everyone, and like many families from multiple cultures, they lovingly weave together an interesting mix of Mexican traditions and indigenous worldview and practices.

No one ever fears my grandparents' discipline. When they indicate we should stop doing something, we just do. There is never any dispute or negotiation, for we know they are guiding us in the correct way, caring for each of us, individually and as part of the family.

I am always comforted by the long, loving hugs from Grandmother and Grandfather Medina as we enter their home. Even as a small child, I wondered how they were able to hug each of us, usually more than forty, for so long. Surely, they would never have enough time to cook, let alone play, sing, and dance, if the hugging continued. Nevertheless, each of us receives that loving look and hug upon entering and upon leaving the family home—and often more hugs in the course of the visit.

On one special occasion, upon both arriving and leaving, my grandmother takes my chubby little hand, saying in Spanish, "*Tu eres la una*," meaning "You are the one." Next, she shows my little hand to my grandfather and, in response, he smiles and gives me an affectionate wink. I am thrilled to be recognized like this! I love to hear my grandfather say, "She is like you, Pachita." Being compared to the beauty and spirit of my grandmother moves me in a powerful way. And my grandmother's phrase, "*Tu eres la una*," remains deep in my heart.

Three and a half decades later, I am journeying to Ecuador for the first time into the high Andes to meet and learn from indigenous Elders.

Early in that trip to the Andes, during a ceremony, a candle burns in front of me, and an Elder comes around the table and takes my hand. Tears begin running down my face, because I can feel a very familiar loving connection that goes beyond his physical hand and the wisdom that shines through his eyes.

I am feeling the spirit of my grandmother, and as he traces and studies my hand, he says, "*Tu eres la una*, you are the one. What are you doing on this side of the table? You should be on the other side, with us."

He continues holding my hand and says, "Your mission in life is to bring more spirit to human beings and to help them take care of the environment. You carry the blood and spirit of the indigenous people, and your work is to bring this spirit of indigenous people into the modern world. You are deepening your connection to indigenous people in Latin America and North America and this will serve you and, more importantly, all of life and all of us, deeply.

"The deep knowing of the wise ones, the healers, is in you. It is important that you came here. You carry the energy of the shaman; the shaman sign shows in your hands. Feel your connection with the jungle, and the mountains, and the connection between the shamans here and your people, your tribes back at home." His words stopped time and called to feelings deep in my heart.

I am called Anita Louise Theresa Medina Sanchez. My name means "graceful warrior." Sometimes I am full of grace and at other times I have a lot to be forgiven. It has been my honor to help connect diverse people from around the world, primarily through global corporations and international nonprofits, to help them recognize and trust their gifts, and to stand together as whole human beings in the power of our connections.

Embracing our similarities and differences, I share the gifts that were given to me and all the people by the Elders to inspire us to live our happiness and highest purpose. Once again, the four gifts are: the power to forgive the unforgivable (and there is a lot to be forgiven); the power of unity, a unity that can make this world a place for all of us, for all species, human, and otherwise; the power of healing, a process that will return us to our essential nature; and the power of hope, the most powerful energy source for positive action.

As humans, we create the institutions that surround us. We must remember that we are human beings and that we can bring human being–ness back into our communities and into these organizations so that they promote love, care, dignity, and collaboration. I want to thank the spirit who created meaning by naming all our relationships, including the sea, the earth, those whose languages we do not speak, and those who have lived here before, the indigenous people of this place.

I was taught to acknowledge the sacred presence of life, and, as a living part of their story, I can feel the presence, the presence of our relations, right here, right now.

If my grandmother Medina, my indigenous *abuelita*, was here, she would . . . oh, but the truth is, she *is* here, drawing a circle on my palm, touching my heart, then moving my hand outward toward you, my new friends, to say thank you for inviting me to be part of your life. *Tu eres la una*, meaning "You are the one." *Nosotros somos los unos*, meaning "We are the ones."

We are the ones—you and I. When Don Coyhis brought his eagle hoop vision to the Elders, they recognized a prophecy—a vision from spirit of one united human race. And as with all prophecies, there's always one last question to ask: When will the prophecy be fulfilled?

In a recent conversation with Elder Ilarion Merculief, he said, "Humans lost track of the present when they invented time." This helps you understand the answer to the above question: The prophecy of the eagle hoop is being fulfilled as you and I take each breath right now. The vision was given from spirit, the Elders heeded the call, and the hoop with one hundred eagle feathers was built, and it continues on its land journey touching thousands of lives. The call to action is arising, such as in the Water Protectors at Standing Rock, in the planting of fifty million trees in a single day in India, in German communities recently opening their doors to more than one million refugees of war, in the international declaration of 598,000 square miles of marine preserves in Antarctic waters, and even by this book. It is being fulfilled as you and I wake up and we unite as one. It is being fulfilled as you and I use these four sacred gifts to be a whole human being who knows we are connected to all life—people, earth, and spirit.

These four gifts are here to support you. You only have to recognize and receive them. You have to stay conscious and awake, choosing to accept and use the gifts in order to step in the circle of life, and live with all your precious relations.

The four gifts are based on pan-Indigenous wisdom and are not bound by borders, race, or religion; they hold the actions to forgive, unify, heal, and give hope. These are true gifts, the forever kind. They have been freely given, and it is an empowering act to receive them. They are meant to be practiced, shared, and then given away over and over and over again to anyone who will receive them—to this generation and to all future generations.

Receive these sacred gifts with an open heart and mind, care for and honor them, and they will deepen your life's abundance and wisdom. Draw on these beautiful and powerful four gifts, discovering all the ways that you can use them, so you can be a life-giving connection to others and yourself as we, together, move into the next phase of life's evolution.

You and I—we are the ones fulfilling the prophecy.

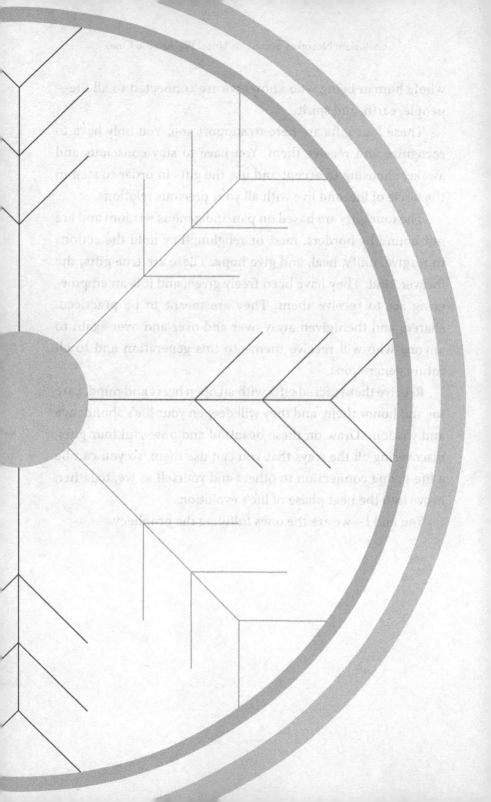

Words of Wisdom from Indigenous Elders of the Four Directions

MY OWN STORY OF awakening to the power of indigenous wisdom was profoundly influenced by the sacred hoop of one hundred eagle feathers. Its co-creation came from the shared intentions and prayers of Elders from the four directions—east, south, west, and north—coming together as a unified call for cooperation and healing between and within cultures.

The four directions depicted in the one hundred eagle feathered hoop and the peoples and the four elements associated with them that are needed to be in harmony and balance for life are:

The East: The yellow direction; keepers of the air—the breath of Life.

The South: The red direction; keepers of the earth—the heart connection and communication with our Mother.

The West: The black direction; keepers of the water—water motion, movement, rhythm, and harmony with the Universe.

The North: The white direction; keepers of the fire (the sun)—the understanding, mastery, and use of Energy.

Out of respect for the sacred hoop and all it represents for humanity, I have asked for prayers of unity from indigenous Elders from around the world in order to share them with you, so that we may celebrate our intimate interconnection. I am very grateful for their generous offering of words of wisdom, kindness, and compassion. May their words and prayers also inspire you and support you in learning from indigenous wisdom, practicing the four gifts, and honoring the original intention of the sacred hoop.

Indigenous cultures are alive and contributing to healing at a global level from all four directions!

THE ELDERS' WORDS

FROM THE EAST: YELLOW DIRECTION

As always, the most important of my *Tai Ji* disciplines is to know when to stop the thinking words and start the dancing.

My spirit takes my mind-body out to my garden and up to my roof studio, to dig my heels into the earth, and to open my arms to the sky. I will gather and scoop in all my assets from outside and from within—I embrace my "tiger and return to my mountaintop." I survey my panoramic vision and shout with my heart full of joy. I kick up my heels and soar. I feel just fine . . . there are no starting and ending numbers on the circle. Life's learnings are ever-expanding circles, always starting from the center within.

—**Chungliang Al Huang, Elder, Author and Founder of the Living Tao Foundation (www.livingtao.org)**

One of the things that we must remember and honor . . . is that there is no separation from human or earth. Through the nomadic perspective, through the spiritual perspective, through the indigenous perspective, we are part of the circle of energy that flows from the land, through the plants, through the animals, through the rocks, through the wind, and then through to humankind.

We all need each other for that interlink, interlinking, interlocking energy. Without it, we are taken out of that environment. If the tree is taken out of that natural environment, if the rock is taken out, if the birds and animals are taken out, they die. The same is what has happened with nomadic human: He is being taken out of that natural environment and he is slowly dying.

Colonialism only considered the physical human; they did not think about the mental, sexual, spiritual, or environmental human. Without his/her land they die.

Our social and economic behavior is dependent on the movement of all weather conditions, and plant and animal behavior. We humankind are the last in this line of changes; we rely on these climatic and ecological conditions to survive.

We need to get our babies back into the bush, and that may be an easy cliché to say but it's got to be tied in with childhood memories, memories to hold the learning of the ways of nature through spiritual connections to the earth.

We've got to give our babies memories and part of these memories, too, is to instill the ability to dream. To learn to dream again about things, about what we're dreaming, and strengthen the ability, so that we continue the dreaming all the time.

In the time that I have on this earth, I would love to see this happen. Get our babies back young and early. We have traditional systems in place, we have the spiritual system as the basis for learning. We can take our children out of school and take them back and start off with what we call "earth stewardship" again.

From this basic beginning, then, we lead on learning about Citizenship, Leadership, and then Eldership. We've got to get these practices instilled in our indigenous society again, so that the kids do have a dreaming pathway, a new dream pathway to follow again. Guided by the Elders and spirits of old people, guided by the stories, we've got to take them back and teach them to reconnect with those spirits—the Spirits of the Land.

—Carol Pettersen, Justice of Peace, Menang/Ngadju Elder
of the Noongar Nation, Western Australia

Shinto traditional prayer and blessing:

Japanese—

けんしょうだいじんつうりき

Pronunciation:

Kensho daijin tsuriki

English Translation:

Oh God, please hear our prayer
And give us your blessings.

—Seikyo Wake (wah-kay: *Wa* means harmony and *ke*
means energy), Japanese Elder and Shinto Priest

There is a very ancient saying about Tibet: "You don't know why, but when you go to Tibet, you feel very peaceful and serene." I always wondered about this. I feel maybe it is because the Tibetan emperor Trisong Detsen decided to bring Buddha's teaching to Tibet in the eighth century.

In short, Buddha's teaching can be summarized as "Wisdom and Compassion." An eagle needs two wings to soar through the sky. (Even a sacred eagle with one hundred feathers still needs two wings.) Likewise, for us, to journey through our infinite lives, we need the wings of both wisdom and compassion, so that we can be wise in every situation and kind, loving, caring, and compassionate to everyone we meet in the infinite journey of our lives.

To shed a little light on what the Enlightened One called Shakya Muni Buddha taught 2,500 years ago in the great land of India regarding "Wisdom and Compassion," he essentially taught that everything is interconnected, interdependent, and dependently arising. Therefore, egocentric-mindedness is baseless, false, and rooted in ignorance. We must go beyond egocentric mind.

Buddha also taught about universal love and infinite compassion. How innately and naturally we, all sentient beings, have this instinct that we want happiness and we don't want any suffering. We, all humanity and all sentient beings, are on this same boat. We must try to, then, help each other physically, emotionally, and spiritually to rise above all suffering and try to find everlasting peace, freedom, and happiness. And we must adopt spiritual principles to not harm anyone verbally, physically, or mentally, and also live a life with the great principles of being kind, caring, and compassionate.

These universal love and compassion teachings have become the dominant force in the Tibetan consciousness for more than a millennium. The mantra for universal compassion, "OM MANI PADME HOONG," is carved on the rocks and printed on prayer flags everywhere in the mountains and villages and chanted by kids to elderly persons in Tibet. His Holiness the Dalai Lama is a personification of Tibetan culture of universal love and compassion. That's what he teaches, that's what he lives for 24/7, that's what he looks for life after life. His favorite prayer is: "For as long as space endures, for as long as suffering sentient beings are there, may I, too, remain until then, to solve their miseries and pains."

In closing, I would love to share with you a kindness phrase blessed and endorsed by ten Nobel Peace Prize laureates, including the Dalai Lama, Desmond Tutu, Rigoberta Menchú Tum (Mayan), Betty Williams, Shirin Ebadi (Iranian), Jody Williams, and others: "May all be kind to each other."

—Nawang Khechog, Tibetan Elder and
Lifelong Student of His Holiness the Dalai Lama
(www.nawangkhechog.com)

FROM THE SOUTH: RED DIRECTION

The world is in turmoil and people wonder what they should do, since it seems like the problems are daunting and overwhelming. What the indigenous Elders say is that we must change our consciousness now, shifting from the mind to the heart. The heart will guide us impeccably. The challenges will not be resolved with logic and reason. It will take trans-rational ways, . . . the ways of the heart.

—Ilarion Merculieff, Unangan Tribe (Aleut),
Global Center for Indigenous Leadership and Lifeways
(www.gcill.org)

Manitou
Wii chi hi shi naam
Chii nii ga moo nung.

———

Great spirit
Guide us to drum
To sing out our voices.

—Ma-Nee Chacaby,
Two-Spirit Ojibwa-Cree Elder, Canada

O:nen kénh nityonkwè:take' tenyethinonhwerá:ton' tsi nón: we' yonkwarihwa'né:konh tetkarihwayeronníhne karihwanoron-hsera'kó:wa Kanonhwaró:ri. Ne' tkayé:ri' tsi orihwakwé:kon yorihwayerihonhátye' ne ní:yoht tsi énhs yethinyahé:sa's ayethi-ya'takenhnhónhake' ne tetsyakoyà:takon's kentho onhwentsyá:ke' teyonkwatawén:rye. O:nen nón:wa' étho tentewawenná:seron' entewarihwá:neke' orihwakwé:kon á:se enwá:ton enkarihwakát-steke' ohén:ton yawenonhátye' ne ní:yoht tsi shiyonhwentsyà: sehkhwe'. Eh káti nenyotonháke ne onkwa'nikón:ra'.

So now we, this assembled group of people, give thanks that everything on earth that we beseeched at the last marked time of midwinter continued to fulfill its duties in the way that the re-maining people depend on them for our survival. It is there then that we layer our words. In the coming days ahead, we humbly request everything to be strengthened—to become as fresh as it was when the world was new. So let it be that way in our minds.

**—Tehota'kerá:tonh (Jeremy Green),
Six Nations Grand River Territory, Ohsweken, Canada;
Excerpt from Stirring-Ashes Speech (Mohawk)**

Sacred K'at. Spiritual secretary of my heart of Heaven, heart of Mother Earth, receive this offering that is your food and gladness, set me free of mental prisons in my life, in my way, in the line of duty.

Allow me to be able to release negative energies from my body and my heart, as the volcanoes cleanse the waters to be drinkable.

Set me free, Sacred K'at, from restrictions of my mind and heart. Then I will be free to share my inner peace and to shelter others in the Web of Love that you represent, Sacred K'at.

Open my way of reconciliation with my family, my neighbors. Keep my family inside the Web of Love.

Make me an instrument of peace to open paths of reconciliation and tolerance in my community, in my country, and this Sacred Planet that is our home.

Send us the connections of love and understanding, so that together we rebuild the Web (K'at) of Respect for Mother Earth with all the original peoples of the world.

—Nana María Chiqui Ramirez, Ayq'ij, Mayan
Timekeeper, Guatemala

Oración al Ajaw en el sagrado espiritu de Kat. (red, enredo, poder de agrupar)

Secretario espiritual de mi Ajaw del cielo recibe esta sagrada ofrenda para regocijarte en tu trono celestial. Espiritu de Kat que no hayan carceles espirituales en mi vida, ni en el camino en el cumplimiento de mi deber. Que no caiga en las injusticias de los hombres, que yo no sea objeto de involucramiento en la injusticia de la gente. Que no me vea encarcelado bendito Kat por la envidia o el egoismo. Concedeme el desarrollo de mis bienes y el desarrollo de mis hijos e hijas. Que sea capaz de liberar las energías negativas de mi cuerpo como los sagrados volcanes liberan su energía para conservar las aguas bebibles. Liberame sagrado Kat de las ataduras de mi mente y mi corazón.

KAT: Red, enredo, poder de agrupar, que ata y / o libera, red que guarda el Sagrado Maíz, el tzukel(feto) en el vientre. Fortalecimiento de las Comadronas, liberación de las ataduras de la mente y el corazón, liberación de las cárceles espirituales y materiales. Dia para pedir la protección para liberarnos de todo obstaculo y/o enredo. Se ofrenda para pedir por las mujeres embarazadas.

—Written by Nana María Ramirez,
Grupo Waxaq'ib Q'ojoom, El Sonido Ceremonial Maya;
Translated by Marisa Meléndez

A *Naku* invitation by the Sápara Nation, emissaries and guardians of the spirit life of the Amazon rain forest:

> *Before there was day, before there was night, the world was*
> *one;*
> *the world was spirit.*

Naku, which means "forest" in the Sápara language, is an urgent call to the world to heal the spirit world and, by virtue of this, to heal us all. It is a call to all our human sisters and brothers to reimmerse ourselves in this great spirit ecology; to allow us once again to be nourished by it as we play our role in sustaining and caring for it.

We invite you to come and experience the reality of the spirit world in person. Encountering the spirit world personally, through dreams, through walks in the forest, and through an intimate connection with the animals and especially plants of our forest, can help slough off the habituated sense of self that stifles the soul when one gets too caught up in the trappings of the material world.

—Manari Ushigua, Emissary and Guardian of the
Sápara Nation of Ecuador (www.naku.com.ec)
(In recognition of the important role we play as
emissaries of the spiritual world of the forest, our culture
and language have been declared Oral and Intangible
Heritage of Humanity by UNESCO.)

More than ever, we need to remember that the earth is our Mother. We have been hurting our own Mother. We must be fully aware—fully aware—that when we drink a glass of water, when we eat our food, that this was given to us by our Mother. It is very important, very necessary at this time, that we humans return to a child-mother relationship. By talking to Mother Earth, by being with her, by giving thanks to her. By crying to her when we need her nourishment. As long as we learn again and practice again, to have a good relationship with Mother Earth, there is hope that we may continue being here.

—Arkan Lushwala, Indigenous Peruvian Spiritual
Teacher, Ceremonial Leader, Healer, and Author of
*The Time of the Black Jaguar: An Offering of Indigenous
Wisdom for the Continuity of Life on Earth*

The time for bringing together the Medicines of the Great Hoop of Life has come. It is a time that has been prophesied by peoples all around Mother Earth for a long, long time, and so we can open our hearts to hope.

Our ancestors preserved this medicine for us by giving

each people, and perhaps we could say, each person, a piece of the whole, thereby the application of such powerful Medicine, could only be accessed in the appropriate way: with all of us standing together, as One Mind, One Heart, One Prayer, One Beautiful Sweet Mother Earth.

As a deeply traumatized species, among many at this point, it seems we will each be faced with the opportunity to forgive the unforgivable, which has been the key to retrieve the heart and truth for me. Any and all methods, practices, for achieving forgiveness are critical at this time. The Medicine released into the world, into Life, Light and Love, that comes with authentic forgiveness, can be likened to the mirror-twin, the opposite, of an atom bomb, an exponential infusion of Grace and Light radiation into the world, penetrating all barriers, affecting every element of Creation.

The greater the hardship, the greater the atrocity, the greater the potential for Medicine to be administered. This is not the ideal "currency" by which to receive this Holy Gift of Life, but in our current status, it is a great possibility that every one of us has at our disposal at this time to make a great contribution to the mending of the Hoop, and to the continuance of beauty for the next seven generations. We are not, and can never be, lone individuals. We are the sum total of our actions as a species, and this is why we can leave nobody out. We, as a species, holding one part of the Hoop of Life, are responsible for upholding that part. If we do not, the Hoop begins to fail. The Hoop of Life does not understand "us and them," the Hoop of Life only understands "We." When we get confused, we can remember a very simple equation: Truth = Life. Any action, intention, prayer that any one of us makes that is for Life automatically makes you a revolutionary on behalf of our kind!

My prayer is to be able to act in every moment in a way that upholds the tremendous honor of being a Human Being. I stand beneath the Holy Father Sun, living star, and all the ancient Star-Beings, and all that is Beyond, on an endlessly Creative Mother Earth, ceaselessly blessing Life, with my Relatives, the Swimming Ones, the Flying Ones, the Creepy-Crawly Ones, the Four-Legged Ones, the Standing Nation (trees), the ancient Waters of Life, perfect in my design to receive this Sacred Gift of thriving Life. I want the Stars to see that I know this is who I am, and this is who we are. I want to Live, really Live, with ALL my relatives. Show us the Truth. Show us what real Love is. I am willing.

We were born into beauty, as beauty, for joyful, thriving Life. That is the Truth. In beauty it is finished. In beauty it is finished. In beauty it is finished. In beauty it is finished.

—Pat McCabe, Weyakpa Najin Win
(Woman Stands Shining), Diné (Navajo) Nation
(www.thrivinglife.weebly.com)

FROM THE WEST: BLACK DIRECTION

Sawubona (Zulu Greeting):

Sawubona says, We see you, and the response is *Yabo Sawubona*: Yes, we see you, too. Because it's a dialogue, seeing is a dialogue. It establishes you as a witness to some phenomenon that can also be a witness to your own presence.

When two human beings meet in this gesture of *Sawubona*, the acknowledgment is we see each other. That becomes an agreement, because we are obligated from that point to affirm the reality that seeing has empowered us to investigate our mutual potential for life. So it invites us to communicate: Why are we? If we are seeing each other, why are we here at the same time? What is this moment of time giving us, to be able to do?

It is an invitation to participate in each other's lives. Seeing, *Sawubona*, also obligates a person to give to each other what's needed for that moment of life to be enhanced.

—Orland Bishop, Elder, Carrier of Zulu Tradition of
South and West Africa, Founder and Director of Shade
Tree Multicultural Foundation (www.shadetreemcf.org)

Batswana (people from Botswana) like to express themselves in proverbs to emphasize truths based on experiences through life. When a Motswana (one Motswana) wants to clarify a point, the first thing that comes to mind is the appropriate proverb to get that point across.

Motho ke motho ka batho, meaning "I am because you are," is a popular and commonly used Setswana proverb or saying. It is also one of my favorite sayings, and this is why I want to share it with you. (Note: Literally it means "A person is a person because of people.")

Unfortunately for me, the saying loses its meaning in translation. Former president of South Africa Mr. Nelson Mandela states: *Motho ke motho ka batho* means "A person is a person through other persons. I am because you are." The saying has been used to explain the importance of our interconnectedness as a people, the idea being that our behaviors and decisions will affect the lives of others and vice versa, creating an invisible thread through which we are all linked. Pull on that thread and you may not feel the difference, but you will inevitably shift the position of others who are also attached.

One of the most debilitating societal problems is the isolation often experienced by many in our communities: the elderly, the mentally ill, and even children. Therefore, it is up to communities to work hard to build this interconnectedness among themselves. It is my hope that by practicing this concept of *Motho ke motho ka batho* we may build safer, stronger, and more caring communities. All people should be able to enjoy communities that provide them with a sense of belonging and a sense of purpose.

It is our duty as people to pull together to strengthen our communities because: *Motho ke motho ka batho*, a person is a person through other persons; and I am because you are.

—**Constance Seloi Bond, Grandmother,**
Mochudi, Botswana

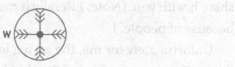

"Sacred Prayer"

Agoo! Agoo! Agoo!
Knock! Knock! Knock!
Father, Mother, God!
Sun, Moon, and Mother Earth
Give us your undivided attention!
In our fractured world and separation from
one another
And from our primordial roots
Alienation from you is inherently false thinking.
May we remember to reconnect with you in
Body, mind, and spirit.
Eyes but no eyes; and ears but no ears
Father, Mother, God forgive us of our
Ignorance of our relationship
To Mother Earth, our joy and happiness.
Sense of guilt, shame. Worry and fear are not
Our inheritance.
Let us find water when we dig.
May peace, love, and happiness be bestowed upon us
today and every day
May eternal love and happiness be with our children,
those who came before us

And those yet to be born always!
Hiao, Ashe, Amen

—Kokomon Clottey, Elder Ga-Adagbe Tribe, Ghana,
West Africa; Musician, Peace Worker (www.kokomon.us)

FROM THE NORTH: WHITE DIRECTION

"Poem on Sami Rights"

Sami rights are fairly easy to comprehend.
Only three rights are in question:
The right to a past
The right to a present
The right to a future

———

The right to one's past is fairly easy to comprehend
Only three rights are in question
The right to experience the memories
The right to respect and appreciate them
To have others treat the memories with respect

———

The right to a present is fairly easy to comprehend
Only three rights are in question
The right to live in peace
The right to make a living
The right to a life of dignity

———

The right to a future is fairly easy to comprehend
Only three rights are in question
The right to leave echoes
To know that these will also be able to leave theirs
The right to have hope and dreams.

—Ánde Somby, Sami Elder

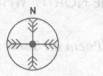

Conversation with Don Coyhis, Mohican Elder and Keeper of the Hoop

IT IS SEPTEMBER 2016. I have driven to Colorado Springs to meet with Don Coyhis, Mohican Elder and keeper of the Eagle Hoop. It's been twenty-two years since we last met at the ceremony when the four gifts were first presented.

We greet each other with a huge hug. He is in jeans and a white shirt with a jean jacket; his hair is gray and tied back in a ponytail. His eyes are smiling behind his wire-rimmed glasses.

As we sit with our coffee, I share with him how the gifts have impacted my life for these past years, and how the gifts from the Elders are now being written about in my book. He smiles and says, "Without you saying anything else, I can tell that this book is coming from spirit. It is time and you are the messenger. I am pleased. How can I be of help?"

ANITA: A lot has happened in the past decades. I want to listen to what you wish to share about the hoop, its journey, your journey, and the journeys of the communities whose lives the wisdom of the Elders has touched.

DON: It is critical for the indigenous communities and all communities to be restored to their health and wholeness. In 1994, when the Hoop was created and the Elders selected those four specific gifts, it became clearer that all the gifts are critical for humankind to live well, knowing our connection to all—earth, people, and spirit. It also became clear that its power for the people grew as the prayers grew; bundles were offered by individuals and whole communities. The hoop is an evolving symbol for humanity, as its wisdom and presence remind us of how to be and how to do. It became clear that after twenty years the hoop was in need of cleansing of the feathers and ribbons to continue its journey of reminding people of who we are, individually and collectively.

In the last year, we had an indigenous woman, someone who has been living her journey facing the trials and the good times with an open heart and faithful spirit of what it means to be a whole human being. She does ceremony, prayers, and song; she was asked to go and cleanse the hoop and prepare it for the time now for women to lead again in the way they have for many tribes. It is not about men not being needed or present; rather, it is the woman who holds the tribe and knows not just from facts but from her connection, intuitively, to spirit where we are to walk.

We call her Mother Earth, not father earth. We call on the

grandmothers, daughters, and granddaughters of the people and of all species to connect us to wellness and to balance with all life. So she took two weeks carefully in prayer and ceremony as she cleansed each feather, unwrapping the ribbons and putting on new ribbons, and in the center a new feather was placed along with a small feather representing the lost indigenous women of Canada, lost women from the United States, and now we know the women from around the world that this violence is happening to. So now the hoop has 102 feathers. It is complete for now.

And the Elders and I and others do not know where all of this is going, what other changes may come. However, we are clear that the symbol, the power of the hoop, and those four gifts are the wisdom needed for this time to support, to be a part of the great shift.

Each time we go into a community with the hoop, we let the people know that the secrets will come out. The secrets must come out of the suffering, violence against women and children; the perpetrators will become known and our work is to stop the needless suffering. And it is hard work and as we do the work the use of the gifts does create more healing, well-being, and happiness.

It also became clear a few years ago that forgiveness is a powerful gift and that there are different kinds of forgiveness that are needed. Perhaps harder even than forgiving the perpetrator of violence is to forgive oneself. So, the Elders felt the call from spirit to create a staff with thirty-six eagle feathers that leads the hoop from where the first feather was placed on it in the fall of 1994. We are seeing different types of healing at the physical, emotional, mental, and spiritual level happening for individuals. We are now sensing from communities that it will take an even greater commitment to live in community as whole human beings, and we are in conversation about whether a community is willing to take on the fullness of "well-briety" for five years.

ANITA: This reminds me of Phil Lane Jr., who talks about the indigenous community in Canada that took a stand and is close to 100 percent sobriety now.

DON: The times have changed and so has our response to each other. It used to be just alcohol consumption that people needed to choose to stop their addiction. Now, like in all communities across this country, and as we hear around the world, the problems are worse with the drugs: meth, heroin, crack cocaine, and more. Men and now women and children are becoming violent and so the need is even greater for the wisdom of the hoop.

ANITA: I see the problems growing greater and I do see the circles starting to grow. Circles of women and men who are responding by creating relationships that are focused on what is healthy for community and uniting their power, embracing their healthy connections to each other, being in ceremony and gratitude with one another and with the earth.

DON: As we speak, the largest gathering in current time is happening at Standing Rock, North Dakota. Thousands of indigenous people, hundreds of tribes and non-indigenous people, are protesting the destruction of the land and the water by the proposed pipeline. You should watch the YouTube video of the young girl who spoke her truth to the tribe, reminding everyone that we have a role.

ANITA: It is so clear from every direction and part of society that we are part of the biodiversity. Our thoughts and our actions that follow do impact our lives, the lives of those around us, and all the other species and elements. I agree with you that we are seeing Elders rise from all ages in response to balancing our impact on each other.

DON: Anita, "Elder" does not have to do with age. There are old ones that are Elders and there are old ones who are not. There are young people who are Elders. We have to stay open and listen with our hearts to all who are sharing their wisdom like that young girl at Standing Rock.

ANITA: Can you tell us more about the Elders who did come together to create this hoop? Where they are from? How they knew that it was these particular four sacred gifts that were needed to live our connection to all our relations?

DON: It was powerful to have so many Elders come from the various tribes in the United States and Canada along with two from the black direction in Africa who brought their water ceremony, and the Sami from the white direction who are the keepers of the fire, and from Asia, the yellow direction, a Tibetan Elder who was said to be a mentor of the Dalai Lama.

We sat in a circle, sometimes in silence, sometimes in song or prayer in all our different forms, and together we created the hoop with the hundred eagle feathers with the four sacred gifts put inside. Also, part of the original instruction was to go receive the feather of the condor from the people in the south. We sent one of the Elders, who flew down and received from the tribe the condor feather that was placed later into the center of the hoop. Are you familiar with the prophecy of the eagle and the condor?

ANITA: Yes, in my work in South America with the Achuar and Sápara people, dream cultures who live in the depths of the rain forest, I hear them speak of this prophecy. How the eagle people of the north would reach their heightened awareness of the mind, and the condor people of the south would reach their heightened awareness of our connection to the heart and to the earth. The eagle people and the condor people cannot survive alone; we need each other. So the prophecy foretold of the time when the eagle and condor would fly together again.

Don, the Elders know—we are all coming to know, through our spirit, science, and relations—that the time has come. We need the wisdom of the indigenous people who are connected to the earth, the heart, and understand how to live in balance with all life; we need the indigenous science of thousands of years that shows us our connection to all life. We are not a hierarchy or simply stewards, we are part of the earth and part of each other. Mass consumption, separation, creating needless suffering left uncheck, will result in more needless suffering, pain and mistreatment, perhaps the end of more species, including our own.

DON: The prophecies of the indigenous people are unfolding. We have an opportunity to heal each other and ourselves; all that we need is here. We have to have the courage and love to move forward.

ANITA: As you speak, I can sense the power of us being connected, understanding we are the One. It is interesting how we do have the ability to hold the paradox of being both an individual and part of the One, the whole.

We are the One; we are abundance. That abundance requires us to accept the responsibility and the joy of knowing everything we think and do has an impact on everything else. It does seem that we need to speed up this awareness. We are hearing more of it on the biological level and physics level about the importance of our biodiversity and how all the elements that are in us are part of the other, too.

DON: Yes, there is much work to do and we need to celebrate, too. The hoop, I will take you to see it and you can put your prayer in it. The hoop reminds the people that we each are sacred and we are all one.

ANITA: Thank you. I am eager to be with the hoop again, especially after all the prayers from the people have been going into it.

We drive to the White Bison office. I enter the wooden door of a multiroom office. The first room is a community room with a simple table, and chairs, and in the corner there stands the hoop.

I can feel the power of the hoop, and immediately am reminded of being in its presence the first time with the hundreds of youth and Elders in 1995. My eyes fill with tears of joy for the wisdom of the Elders and for this majestic hoop of 102 eagle feathers now.

I remain standing just inside the doorway as Don Coyhis lights the sage to cleanse himself to be in the presence of the hoop. He gently places one hand on the hoop and bows his head. I can hear faint words through tears as he prays. Then he turns and with an eagle feather in his hand he signals me over.

The feather first touches each of my hands in order that they be the holder of truth, then my feet so that I walk with humility and strength on the sacred earth. The large eagle feather touches my eyes so that I can see the truth, the beauty, and the pain so as to be able to do what is needed, and then brushes my ears so that I hear the truth and know when it is not the truth, my mouth so that I speak only the truth with compassion, and, lastly, the top of my head so that I be open to receiving the strength and wisdom from spirit.

The sage continues to waft in the air. I ask if I can put my offering from the Amazon rain forest into the hoop's basket of prayers. Don looks as I open my hand, which holds a little bottle of dragon's blood tree sap from one of the many healing trees in the rain forest—an offering from the plant people and the people of the condor. Don gestures and I gently step on the red blanket that holds the hoop and place the healing tree nectar into the basket of offerings.

I can feel Don and the eagle feather in his hand pull away, allowing me to be fully focused on this friend of mine that I had not seen for so long. I gently place both hands on the hoop and fill my heart with gratitude and love for the sacred gifts that have supported me in transforming my life in service and joy. With my eyes slightly open and all my senses softly alert, I chant gratitude to the winds of the four directions. The words fill the room and beyond as my exhales cause several of the eagle feathers to ruffle ever so slightly.

I am reminded that I am home. With Don and his assistants, two beautiful Mohicans, in the room, I am filled with the joy and power of knowing that we are all sacred.

We are the One!

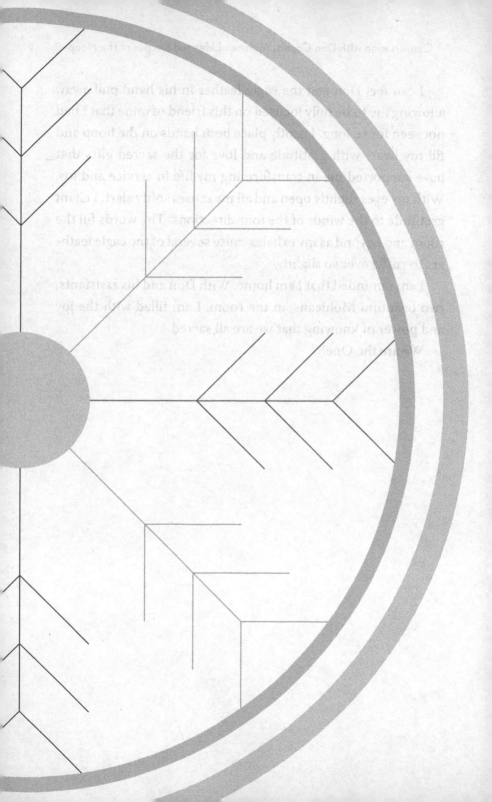

Young People with Old Spirits: Emerging Elders

The prophecy of the seventh generation says that when the seventh generation of young people come, the great winter will end, for these young people with old spirits will lead and make change—a reuniting with each other and with Mother Earth will happen. Out of the thousands who came to stand in solidarity at Standing Rock in North Dakota to protect the earth's sacred water and land for this and future generations, three young indigenous leaders—Jasilyn Charger, age nineteen; Xiuhtezcatl Martinez, age sixteen; and Mia Sage Xillonie Stevens, age twenty-two—share their words of wisdom, hope, and inspiration. They are the four sacred gifts in action.

I am from the River Sioux tribe, located in Eagle Butte, South Dakota. I founded the International Indigenous Youth Council

(IIYC), based out of Standing Rock Reservation in North Dakota. (www.facebook.com/IIYCFamily)

When you really look at the world and its beauty and what it has to offer all of us, of how old it is, how much it has seen, even when history gets lost, the memories are still kept. The earth remembers—it holds our heritage in her heart. All the blood that has been spilled on the ground trying to possess her—it leaves an imprint.

She sees all the wars, all the genocide, and the harm but also the love. Why do we look forward to a heaven we must change ourselves to access, when our Mother Earth created one for us to live peacefully in?

How are we expected to be granted a new home in the afterlife, when we constantly destroy the home we are given in this life?

She shows us life every day.

The beauty we see in nature is the beauty we should see in each other and ourselves in how different we are. No place is the same and no person is the same. Nothing stays the same.

We waste time clinging to a world that isn't ours to keep, instead of making sure it is here for our children to come. My people understood this and they were so kind to think and dream of me. They died and suffered and fought against all odds to make sure I will have a life and give it to my children. Now, that is the legacy that they have passed down to us.

Across the ages, the human race has been at war with itself to stay alive. Why does my generation have to fight to have water, to have food, and a good life, when life is a gift and should be respected?

Because we all die. But we are stronger and more awake and united than we have ever been. Because the children of our enemies are allies now.

We are healing as a race from the historical trauma we all have endured.

We are all indigenous to this planet. We are all related.

—Jasilyn Charger, Cheyenne

At this point in time, we are at war if you choose to call it that. We are battling some of the most powerful and influential companies on the planet. There are twelve- and fourteen-year-old kids going up against multibillion-dollar industries. Because what those companies stand for is power and greed and we come with innocence. We are standing up for our future, for the world that we are going to be left with.

And at this point in time, seeing this as a war is not working. We don't want to go to war. If you say to someone, "Hey, join the war on climate change," who's going to want to do that?

It is a different thing when we say, "Who wants to build solutions for change, to create a better world, a more sustainable world for every generation to come, so that we don't have to keep repeating the same problems that past generations have created? Who wants to help me cultivate the solutions? Who wants to help me find the people who are going to bring forth the answers that we need for every generation to solve some of the greatest issues of our time?"

Some of the greatest minds on earth are part of this generation, and we don't even know it yet. So, yes, we are at war, but *that* is the problem. We are seeing this problem as something to attack. Many are seeking to find something to fight against.

But we will be so much more successful if we ask ourselves: What are we fighting for?

We are fighting for our children. We are fighting for our air and our water. What are we going to do, and how are we going to do that?

This war is not going to be waged with weapons but with the hearts and the minds and the passions of the people of this earth who see that there is a fundamental problem with our society, a fundamental issue with the way that we relate with each other as human beings. There is a fundamental issue with the mind-set we have toward our earth, and when people see that, they will realize the enemy is not the oil and gas industry, or the fossil fuel industry, or climate change itself, but with the way in which humanity is viewing everything around us. We are viewing our planet as a resource, something we can take from, something we can use to gain from.

It seems that even if we were to put laws into place and managed to solve climate change politically, if the change did not come from the people, we would be right back in the same place ten years into the future. There is always going to be something else, unless the change comes from a systemic flip, where we realize that the problem is not how much gas we are taking, or how much we are contaminating our rivers; the problem is that we justify the destruction of our planet because it is convenient, and that is what has to change.

—Xiuhtezcatl Martinez, Aztec-Mexika Tribe,
Founder of Earth Guardians (www.earthguardians.org)

At Standing Rock, I spoke with leader and activist Dolores Huerta, and something she said stuck in my mind: "The young people are always the prophesiers of society." Her words gave me extra hope and faith that we could make it through whatever happens in the future, and it will always be worth it.

One heart, one mind, and one prayer for the ancestors, Elders, youth, and future generations—to unite everyone from every direction and every color to protect the people.

My generation is known as the seventh generation, because we are going to make a change for that eighth fire to stay pure and to set out a path to a better life. I recently joined the International Indigenous Youth Council, where the locals and runners started a prayer to protect the water in North Dakota against an illegal pipeline on treaty land. Other youths, such as myself, joined to help, as we also are facing problems in our own communities.

We united to help each other out; to expand our information, experiences, and knowledge; to survive and conquer these problems in this world. When the camp saw what the youth were doing spiritually and physically, they acknowledged us with a ceremony with the Elders, where they offered us a staff and *chanupa* (peace pipe) that is three hundred years old. We committed our life to the people.

The original runners and youth from Sacred Stone Camp committed with the International Indigenous Youth Council. All the people are uniting from every nation in a time of need. I am honored to be a part of the awakening of the cause every-where. To accept everyone is almost like traditionally adopting everyone.

It's hard to have patience, but we all have something to bring to the table and could all learn from each other. All the Elders have something to offer. There are situations where people all over America are facing the government that we need to be aware of. We have been victims in trauma from the govern-ment, so we're reaching out. My father taught me to not judge, just to gain knowledge: just as there are many rays to the sun, there are as many ways to the Creator.

I am the People, I cry with the People, I am hurt with the People, I heal with the People, I become stronger with the People. I am the People.

—Mia Sage Xillonie Stevens, Mexican and Paiute Tribe

Acknowledgments

How do I adequately give gratitude to the Spirit, Grandmother and Grandfather, the People, and the earth—all the plants, the animals, the water, and other elements? I guess it may be impossible; however, I hear the voice of the Elders say, "Just speak with your heart and there is no judgment, only the pure sound of love."

These friends and relatives, and others unnamed, have accompanied me on this journey. They have been at my side and in my heart. To each of you, my gratitude, love, and blessings for your contribution to my life.

This book could not have taken shape without the love and trust that the indigenous Elders placed in my hands. In particular, I thank Don Coyhis, Mohican, founder and president of White Bison organization, and keeper of the hoop that holds the gifts given from the Elders from the four directions. Gratitude to all the twenty-seven indigenous Elders from the Americas (the Red/Brown direction), two Elders from Africa who contributed their water ceremony (the Black direction), the Elder from the Sami tribe of Finland (White direction), and the Elder from Tibet (Yellow direction). Your collective response to the call from spirit set into motion, and continues to foster, healing, forgiveness, unity, and hope in action for individuals and communities.

Special thanks to all the indigenous Elders who contributed your wisdom, vision, prayers, chants, songs, and ceremonies to this book, oh so lovingly inviting us all to live in harmony with all our relations: Don Coyhis (Mohican), Norbert Hill (Oneida), Eddie Bent Box Sr. (Southern Ute), Henrietta Mann (Southern Cheyenne), Phil Lane Sr. (Yankton Sioux), Phil Lane Jr. (Ihanktonwan Dakota and Chikasaw), Chief Oren Lyons (Seneca Nation of the Iroquois Confederacy), Chungliang Al Huang, Carol Pettersen (Noongar Nation, Western Australia), Seikyo Wake (Shinto, Japan), Nawang Khechog (Tibet), Ilarion Merculieff (Unangan), Ma-Nee Chacaby (Ojibwa-Cree), Tehota'Kerá:tonh (Jeremy Green-Mohawk), Nana María Chiqui Ramirez (Mayan), Manari Ushigua (Sápara), Arkan Lushwala (Peru), Pat McCabe (Diné/Navajo), Orland Bishop (Zulu), Constance Seloi Bond (Mochudi, Botswana), Kokomon Clottey (Ga-Adagbe, Ghana), and Ánde Somby (Sami, Norway). And to all those who have opened my heart and inspired and counseled me on the journey that I have neglected to name. And to the many young leaders—young people with old spirit who are emerging elders: Jasilyn Charger (Cheyenne), Mia Sage Xillonie Stevens (Mexican and Paiute), and Xiuhtezcatl Martinez (Aztec-Mexika).

Many thanks to the editors who helped me through all the phases of this seven-year writing journey: Emily Han, Geoffrey Berwind, Kit Tennis, Ted Ringer, Haley Weaver, Karen Rudolph, Kathy Sparrow, Mishael Patton, Donna Kozik, Ana Sophia Demetrakopoulos, and Pele Rouge.

Immense gratitude to my cheerleaders and publishers at

Simon & Schuster: at Atria Books, Judith Curr, and at Enliven Books, Zhena Muzyka. We laugh about who really manifested who to bring these messages out to the world. This book would not have been completed without you.

Last, but not least, my family and friends who have supported me, encouraged me, and inspired me to share my truth, strength, and vulnerability on this journey. With love to my husband, Kit Tennis; my sons, Alex and Nico Tennis; my brothers and sisters, Paula, Phil, Olivia, Richard, and Gregory; and my late grandfather, Modesto Medina, and especially my late grandmother, Paula Medina—you are the One, and all my Aztecan and Mexican ancestors. And to my friends, muses, and supporters: Jack Canfield, Patty Aubury, Lynne and Bill Twist, Claude and Noelle Poncelet, Dr. Deb Sandella, Karin Roest, Rachel Marco-Havens, Lin Morel, Isaac and Thorald Koren—the Kin, Robert Gass, Steve Harrison and his Quantum Leap team, Bob and Cynthia Chapman and the Massive 2012 friends, Norbert Hill and all the friends and Elders at the American Indian Science and Engineering Society and at White Bison, and all my partners at the Pachamama Alliance and the Bioneers organization.

And love and gratitude to all my relations: human beings, all the birds (especially the eagles), the rain forest, the waters of the Amazon, the trees, the volcanoes, the mountains, the mountain lions, the bears, the four winds, and the Spirit of Life itself.

In gratitude for their critically important work and their lasting influence on my life, I am dedicating a portion of my author royalties from this book to the nonprofits American Indian Science and Engineering Society (www.aises.org) and White Bison (www.whitebison.org).

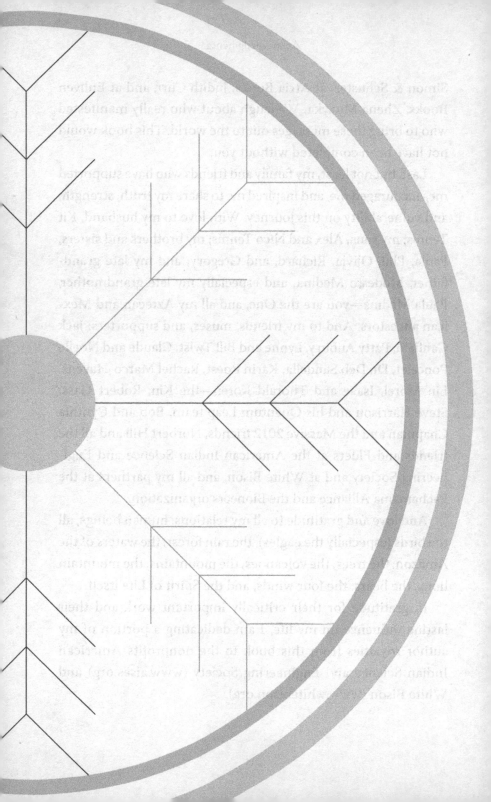

Notes

1. Chief Oren Lyons, statement given at Bioneers board of directors meeting, San Francisco, March 2015.
2. First People: The Legends. "Native American Legends: Cherokee Prophecies." Accessed December 9, 2016. http://www.firstpeople.us /FP-Html-Legends/Cherokee_Prophecies-Cherokee.html.
3. Phil Lane Jr., "Indigenous Wisdom for Compassionate Living & Unified Action." Notes from online class. The Shift Network, January 7, 2015.
4. Walmart: Sustainability. "Twenty First Century Leadership." Accessed December 9, 2016. http://corporate.walmart.com/_news_/executive -viewpoints/twenty-first-century-leadership.
5. Alice Walker, *In Search of Our Mothers' Gardens: Womanist Prose* (San Diego: Harcourt, 1983), 242–43.
6. Phil Lane Jr., "Indigenous Wisdom for Compassionate Living & Unified Action." Notes from online class. The Shift Network, January 7, 2015.
7. Wangari Maathai, acceptance speech for the Nobel Peace Prize. Oslo City Hall, Oslo, Norway, 2004.
8. Chief Oren Lyons, statement given at Bioneers board of directors meeting, San Francisco, March 2015.
9. Václav Havel, *Disturbing the Peace: A Conversation with Karel Huizdala* (New York: Vintage, 1991), 181–82.
10. Joe Kane, *Savages* (New York: Knopf, 1995), 9.
11. Ibid., 76.